JEWISH ENCOUNTERS

Jonathan Rosen, General Editor

Jewish Encounters is a collaboration between Schocken and
Nextbook, a project devoted to the promotion of Jewish literature, culture, and ideas.

>nextbook

PUBLISHED

FORTHCOMING

A Fine Romance

DAVID LEHMAN

A FINE ROMANCE

Jewish Songwriters, American Songs

NEXTBOOK · SCHOCKEN · NEW YORK

Grateful acknowledgment is made to the following for permission
to reprint previously published and unpublished material:
Alfred A. Knopf and Brad Leithauser: Excerpt from "A Good List" from *Curves
and Angles: Poems* by Brad Leithauser, copyright © 2006 by Brad Leithauser.
Reprinted by permission of Alfred A. Knopf and Brad Leithauser.
Alfred Publishing Co., Inc.: Excerpt from "War Song" by Cole Porter,
copyright © by Chappell & Co., Inc. (ASCAP). All rights reserved.
Reprinted by permission of Alfred Publishing Co., Inc.
Commentary: Excerpts from "Jerome Kern and American Operetta" by Kurt List
(*Commentary*, May 1947). Reprinted by permission of *Commentary* magazine.
The Literary Estate of May Swenson: Excerpt from "An Exuberance,
Not a Dump" by May Swenson. Reprinted by permisson of Carole Berglie,
executor of the Literary Estate of May Swenson.
Sony/ATV Music Publishing LLC: Excerpts from "Love Is Just Around the
Corner" by Leo Robin, copyright © 1934 by Sony/ATV Harmony.
All rights reserved. Reprinted by permission of Sony/ATV Music
Publishing LLC, 8 Music Square West, Nashville, TN 37203.

Library of Congress Cataloging-in-Publication Data
Lehman, David, [date]–
A fine romance : Jewish songwriters, American songs /
David Lehman.
p. cm.
Includes bibliographical references.
ISBN 978-0-8052-4250-8
1. Popular music—United States—History and criticism.
2. Popular music—United States—Jewish influences.
3. Jewish composers—United States.   4. Jewish lyricists—United States.
I. Title.
ML3477.L45 2009
782.42164089'924073—dc22   2009005942

www.schocken.com
Printed in the United States of America
First Edition
2 4 6 8 9 7 5 3 1

For Stacey

TIME AFTER TIME

CONTENTS

APOLOGIA

Little White Lies

And heaven was in your eyes.

WALTER DONALDSON, "Little White Lies"

M ark Twain opens *The Adventures of Huckleberry Finn*
with a disclaimer. Huck, the narrator, says that readers of *The Adventures of Tom Sawyer* have already encountered
him. "That book was made by Mr. Mark Twain, and he told
the truth, mainly. There was things which he stretched, but
mainly he told the truth."

In the book you have before you, the author has likewise
endeavored to tell the truth, mainly, about a subject close to
his heart. *A Fine Romance* is conceived, in Huck Finn's words,
as "mostly a true book, with some stretchers." The stretchers occur principally in the narrator's autobiography and in
accounts of his relatives and friends.

Otherwise, this is a work of nonfiction. Every detail
about the songwriters is, to the best of the author's knowledge, accurate.

A Fine Romance

PRELUDE

Jewish Genius

I'll write Jewish tunes.

COLE PORTER

That Old Black Magic

Whether you date the genesis to Irving Berlin and "Alexander's Ragtime Band" in 1911 or to Jerome Kern and "They Didn't Believe Me" in the first year of the Great War, sooner or later you have to explain what is Jewish about American popular song—apart from the simple fact that a great many of the songwriters were Jews. A lot of it has to do with sound: the minor key, bent notes, altered chords, a melancholy edge. Even happy songs sound a little mournful. Marian McPartland is at the piano playing George Gershwin's "Love Walked In" as I walk in on her, and though the words say that love has driven all the shadows away, it's the sound of the shadows and their echoes that I hear, and in my mind, Ira's tender love lyric is really a tear-filled good-bye, and I think of his brother's early death and how sad and lonely a man George would have been if he'd had his brother's introspective nature. Anyone who doubts that there is a distinctively Jewish character to, say, Gershwin's music or Berlin's or Harold Arlen's should listen to "Someone to Watch Over Me" (lyrics Ira Gershwin) and "Let's Face the Music and Dance" (lyrics Irving Berlin), and "Stormy Weather" (lyrics Ted Koehler), respectively. It's there in the plaintive undertow, the feeling that yearning is eternal and sorrow not very far from the moment's joy. You can hear it at the end of the bridge (or "release") in "Stormy Weather." The wish to "walk in that sun once more" occurs like a religious epiphany, an exclamatory instant of elation in a bluesy prayer that modulates from complaint to resignation.

Or consider the rhymes in Berlin's invitation to the dance as suavely and persuasively sung by Fred Astaire. "Let's Face the Music and Dance" begins with a forecast of "trouble ahead." Soon enough we won't have the music and moonlight that lead to love and romance. After "the fiddlers have fled," we'll have to pay the bill. Tomorrow is scary, "with teardrops to shed," and our one consolation is today. No dance invitation ever sounded so threatening. It's time to "face the music" in both senses—to face the facts, no matter how disturbing, and they are plenty disturbing in the Depression year of 1936, *and* to face your partner and dance, dance defiantly, regardless of the bad news breaking in Germany, Spain, Italy, and the rest of Europe. That double meaning is a grand example of Berlin's wizardry: He doesn't avoid clichés, he embraces them and gives them new life. The popular songs that Jewish songwriters wrote were ones that Americans of all ethnicities and every brow level (high, middle, low) could sing along with and dance to.

In *The House That George Built*, his homage to Gershwin, Berlin, Arlen, et al., Wilfrid Sheed uses the key phrases "Jewish music" and "Jewish songs." The nearest he comes to defining either term is when he speaks of "the mystery ingredients of jazzness and bluesness," which enabled a certain decidedly non-Jewish songwriter of sophistication and élan to surpass himself.[1] In an appreciation of Harold Arlen on the centenary of his birth in 2005, John Lahr makes a similar association. In addition to "crazy jazz," Lahr writes, Arlen's sound "incorporated the Jewish wail and the wail of the blues."[2] This line of thinking goes back to Gershwin, who felt that jazz sprang from "the negro spiritual" and that "the American soul" combines "the wail, the whine and the exultant note of the old mamy [*sic*] songs of the South. It is black and white. It is all colors and all souls unified in the great melting-pot of the world. Its dominant note is vibrant syncopation."[3]

Let's begin, then, with the mysterious "bluesness" and "crazy" jazz that links Jewish songwriters tonally and rhythmically with black singers and instrumentalists. Can you hear the wail? It fills the air when the clarinet glissando kicks off Gershwin's *Rhapsody in Blue*. Nor can you miss it in Arlen's early collaborations with lyricist Ted Koehler: "Let's Fall in Love" and "Between the Devil and the Deep Blue Sea" and "I Gotta Right to Sing the Blues," several of them written when Arlen and Koehler were house musicians at the Cotton Club in Harlem. If anything, the Jewishness of

Arlen's songs enhances their appeal for a soulful non-Jewish performer (the white Lee Wiley, the black Billie Holiday), who can insinuate the sound of heartbreak into a declaration of love. The on-again, off-again love affair between Jewish songs and black musicians in particular is not an uncomplicated one. But it's an important part of the story, evident not only in jazz standards written by Jews and interpreted by blacks (as when Art Blakey and the Jazz Messengers play Harold Arlen's "Come Rain or Come Shine"), but in such landmark theatrical events as *Show Boat* in 1927 (music Jerome Kern, lyrics Oscar Hammerstein) and *Porgy and Bess* in 1935 (music George Gershwin, lyrics Ira Gershwin and DuBose Heyward) in which African American characters are, on one level, allegorical representations of Jews.

Whenever *Show Boat* and *Porgy and Bess* are revived, it is always a noteworthy event and often one that sparks some protest. Some critics resent what they consider the white and specifically Jewish appropriation of the lives of the blacks of Catfish Row in *Porgy and Bess*. Others object to the perpetuation of racial stereotypes. The fact that minstrel shows played a vital part in the development of American popular song is a retrospective embarrassment. The sight of Al Jolson in blackface in *The Jazz Singer* or Fred Astaire in blackface as Bojangles of Harlem in *Swing Time* requires explanation and apologia. But protests reflect the temper of their age and these misgivings are likely to fade; the excellence of the music and the honor and dignity it confers on performer and audience alike will have trumped all other considerations. When the black male chorus in *Show Boat* reaches the end of the second verse of "Ol' Man

River"—the part where the singers can envision the river Jordan, the "old stream" that they long to cross—it is a visionary moment, and Kern's majestic music makes you feel that unreachable heaven looms near as a prayer or a worker's dream of liberation from "the white man boss." As Hammerstein's peroration climbs in keeping with Kern's music, the human condition is humbly stated. The song ennobles singer and listener not because it acknowledges that failure is our common lot—we are all sick of trying, tired of living, and scared of dying—but because we are moved to sing about it with robust voices and to celebrate something greater than ourselves: the natural wonder of the Mississippi River that just keeps rolling along, powerful and timeless, like a divinity. At such a "moment divine" (to use a Hammerstein phrase from another standard he wrote with Kern), you almost feel that the Jewish songwriters and black performers have achieved a momentary but transcendent fusion of identities.

The Jewish element in American popular song is a property not only of the notes and chords but of the words as well, or, more exactly, the union between words and music. Perennially regarded as secondary partners—the way Lorenz Hart was to Richard Rodgers or Ira Gershwin to his younger, taller genius brother, George—the lyricists had their own order of greatness. It could be said that they followed a Jewish imperative in their abundant humor, wit, and cleverness and in their ability to mix sadness and elation and to produce thereby the mysterious tingle of romance.[4] I'm prepared even to argue that the great American standards— such as "Blue Skies," "The Lady Is a Tramp," "I Got

Rhythm," "The Way You Look Tonight," "My Funny Valentine," "Tea for Two," "Love Me or Leave Me," "All the Things You Are," "Over the Rainbow," and "I've Got You Under My Skin"—are in some fundamental way inflected with Judaism even when the composer or the lyricist was neither by birth nor conviction Jewish. (Only one song of the ten I just mentioned was entirely the work of a non-Jew, and he acknowledged that he was "writing Jewish.") Whether performed by Sinatra or Ella, Bing or Peggy Lee, Benny Goodman or Miles Davis, the songs celebrated, bewailed, orchestrated, and maybe even enacted a romance—a fine romance, though one sometimes lacking in kisses or other signs of requital or affection. Some cases merited sarcasm, as in Dorothy Fields's lyric for a delightful Kern tune that Ginger Rogers and Fred Astaire sing in *Swing Time.* No clinches, no pinches; you won't nestle or wrestle. I never "muss the crease in your blue serge pants," Rogers laments. It's a fine romance nevertheless. And what a sexy line that is. Miss Fields got Mr. Kern to swing—not altogether an easy thing.

"I'll take romance." "Our romance won't end on a sorrowful note." "I know that music leads the way to romance." "Here's to my first romance." "Isn't it romantic?"[5] "Romance" and "romantic" recur as they do not only because "romance" rhymes with "dance" and because so many songs are variations or elaborations of "I love you" but for a third reason combining the other two. The Jewish songwriters, in their lives and works, were conducting a passionate romance with America—from initial attraction to courtship, consummation, joy, disenchantment, despair, and then the whole sequence over again. As in all such affairs there were ups and downs. The promised land of America promised more than it could deliver. In "Ten Cents a Dance," the song that launched Ruth Etting's singing career, Lorenz Hart cleverly rhymes "hero" with the middle syllables of "queer romance." The song represents the point of view of a dance-hall hostess, whom men—"pansies" as well as "rough guys"—"rent" on a cash basis. If she has a romance with a ticket-buying would-be "hero," it is going to be "queer" in the sense of odd. In Hart's own case, both meanings of "queer" apply. As a homosexual at a time when you had to conceal the fact, Hart—self-conscious to begin with because he was barely five feet tall and thought himself ugly—suffered and drank. The romance for him came to a self-destructive end. He died in despair at forty-eight. But the frustration and pain equipped this naturally ebullient punster to write great lyrics that combine sadness with lust. The writer Jerome Lawrence made an astute observation about Richard Rodgers's first writing partner. "You can name many artists who constantly fight their unworthiness, but Larry Hart articulated it more than almost anybody," Lawrence said. "Because of being a songwriter he had to write love songs, and almost all his love songs said, 'I stink. Why would you ever love me? Spring is here, I hear, but for other people, not for me.' He was the poet laureate of masochism."[6]

Perhaps only a disillusioned enthusiast could produce such effects of anguish without sinking into sentimentality or self-pity. But then, the American romance in popular song exerts its pull because, in Ira Gershwin's words, the romance "won't end on a sorrowful note," though end it must. It would be an illusion to think otherwise, but what's wrong with that? Art relies on illusion. Illusions, including the illusion of timeless truths and undying love, are a necessary part of any imaginative strategy for dealing with and maybe even redeeming the failures of experience, the insufficiency or inadequacy of actuality. "My Romance," another Rodgers and Hart song, rises to the defense of illusions. A song is an abbreviated vision or waking dream, a statement of desire and a supposition of its fulfillment. "My Romance" praises the power to make one's "most fantastic dreams come true." All that the romance needs is "you"—that most flexible of pronouns, more intimate than any other, conveniently genderless, masking rather than naming the beloved, and yet so powerfully immediate that the word can stand as easily for an unknown or an imaginary personage as for the flesh-and-blood creature with whom you are, right now, dancing in the dark or dancing cheek to cheek.

The Jewish songwriter had an extra incentive to participate in this aesthetic adventure: He or she, an outsider, universally despised for reasons racial and religious, was getting to compose the music and words of the insider's dream. This was America, where almost everybody could feel like an outsider, a newcomer to the inheritance, and where the technological marvels of the modern age—the radio and the telephone, the movies, the microphone, the long-playing record, the television set—welcomed and rewarded originality and enterprise in the popular arts. John Bush Jones wrote a book winningly called *The Songs That Fought the War* about the value of popular music on the home front during

World War II. The songs did fight in the ideological battle, the propaganda war; they sold bonds on the one hand and on the other offered consolation to the lonely and daydreams of nights on the town after our boys took Berlin. That was how a lyricist like Frank Loesser ("Praise the Lord and Pass the Ammunition") or Sammy Cahn ("It's Been a Long, Long Time") contributed to the war effort. But whatever the stated content of the songs, they served as linkages, messages between the soldier abroad and the people back home. They conveyed the romance of illusions. And if you heard the strains of "But Beautiful" or "You and the Night and the Music" and there were ladies present and a friendly bartender, people would spontaneously begin to dance as if it were the most natural thing in the world. (Think of all the movies in which this happens.) *The songs made people dance.* And the dance, the conventional fox-trot or old-fashioned waltz, acquired, in Arlene Croce's phrase, a "special luminosity . . . as an emblem of sexual union."[7] In a song, "to dance" is code for something more intimate that could not be stated explicitly when concepts like "mixed company" still had currency. As George Bernard Shaw said about dancing, it's "a perpendicular expression of a horizontal desire."[8] It could even be argued that the songs that made people dance were the most important part of the whole dating and mating ritual. Oh, it cast a spell on you, this American romance, irresistible as that old black magic that spins you around and makes you feel like you're in a skyscraper elevator rapidly going down.

The Secret of Writing Hits

I return to my original question: In what sense is urban American popular music a Jewish phenomenon? There is a flip way to make the case. Leave it to Lenny Bruce: "To me, if you live in New York or any other big city, you are Jewish. It doesn't matter even if you're Catholic; if you live in New York you're Jewish." Then there is the "know it when you hear it" school of thought. Virgil Thomson, the composer whose music criticism in the *New York Herald-Tribune* made him one of the nation's leading arbiters, dismissed George Gershwin's "gefilte fish" scoring in *Porgy and Bess.*[9] Whether you regard the comment as a slur or just a colorful way to register a criticism, it makes it plain that Thomson's educated ears picked up the synagogue rather than the indigenous Gullah sound of Charleston, and this meant that the putative folk opera was, in his view, "fake folk-lore."[10] There are more favorable ways of considering the fusion of black and Jewish elements in Gershwin's treatment of the denizens of Catfish Row. But what I want to note here is the assumption, general in the 1920s and 1930s and shared by Thomson, that the "jazz" Gershwin epitomized was, in a phrase, "Africanized Jewish music." In 1941, the music historian John Tasker Howard asserted that jazz was "a Jewish interpretation of the Negro" and added, "What could be more American than such a combination, even though it does ignore those of us who have Puritan ancestors?"[11]

An anecdote in Richard Rodgers's autobiography advances the thesis that the Jewish quality of American popular song is so fundamental—and so unrelated to the actual religion—that you will find it even in the work of the corn-fed Hoosiers (Hoagy Carmichael, Cole Porter) and Savannah songbirds (Johnny Mercer) among the many other white musicians not of the faith (Harry Warren, Vincent Youmans, Walter Donaldson, for starters) who kept up with the Gershwins, the Berlins, and the Kerns.

It was in Venice in 1926 that Rodgers met Cole Porter, then unknown to him. But Porter knew who Rodgers was. Rodgers and Hart had made it on Broadway. "Manhattan" was the toast of the town. Porter, in contrast, had written the scores of several shows, none of which had, well, scored. According to Rodgers, who often complained about Hart's penchant for disappearing, no sooner did he and his partner reach Venice than the lyricist ditched the composer and headed for the nearest bar. When Dick went for a stroll alone on the Lido, whom should he run into but his old friend Noël Coward, and Noël had a friend in a nearby cabana, and there stood Porter, a "slight, delicate-featured man with soft saucer eyes and a wide, friendly grin." That evening Rodgers and Hart dined with Coward and the Porters, Cole and his wife, Linda, in the Palazzo Rezzonico, the grand palace where Robert Browning had died. Coward had rented it for the season. All through dinner Porter peppered Rodgers with questions. After they ate, they took turns at the piano. When Porter played "Let's Do It" and "Let's Misbehave," Rodgers knew that here was a major talent. He conveyed his enthusiasm, and Porter confided that despite his failures on Broadway, he thought he had finally figured out the secret of writing hits. Rodgers leaned over expectantly. "I'll write Jewish tunes," Porter said. Rodgers laughed at the time, but looking back he realized that Porter was serious and had been right. "Just hum the melody that goes with 'Only you beneath the moon and under the sun' from 'Night and Day,' or any of 'Begin the Beguine,' or 'Love for Sale,' or 'My Heart Belongs to Daddy,' or 'I Love Paris.' These minor-key melodies are unmistakably eastern Mediterranean," Rodgers writes in *Musical Stages*. "It is surely one of the ironies of the musical theatre that despite the abundance of Jewish composers, the one who has written the most enduring 'Jewish' music should be an Episcopalian millionaire who was born on a farm in Peru, Indiana."[12] Though Rodgers doesn't spell it out, it is easy enough to understand that Porter, the gay Yalie, may have had more than one thing in common with the New York Jewish boys who went to Columbia. Do what Rodgers suggested. Listen to Mary Martin sing "My Heart Belongs to Daddy"—to that part of the song where she says "Da" and repeats the syllable eight times. What you get is a patter of baby talk, or fake baby talk, and a pun on "Dada." But if you slow down the tempo you also hear the sound of lamentation in the temple on the Ninth of Av: da da da, da da da, da da da. Can you hear it? To my ears, "What Is This Thing Called Love?" (as Frank Sinatra sings it on his album *In the Wee Small Hours of the Morning*) and the lesser-known masterpiece "Looking at You" (as recorded, unforgettably, by Lee Wiley on April 15, 1940) are as "Jewish" in sound and in attitude as anything by Rodgers, Kern, or Arthur Schwartz. Can you hear the klezmer sound in "I Love Paris"?[13]

There is, then, a sense in which the Judaic component of popular American song stands as an entity unto itself. You didn't have to be Jewish to write "Jewish tunes." As a composer you just needed an ear for it. The cantor's sons and other temple-goers had a natural advantage, of course. They could rely on the praises and lamentations from the liturgy that were buried in their brains. One day I happened to be listening to an Al Jolson record. I had heard many other versions of "Swanee," George Gershwin's first hit, but in Jolson's animated rendition, the first line of the verse sounded different. "I've been away from you a long time." Or rather, it sounded familiar in an uncanny way. What was it? And then I remembered the Sabbath prayer: *Hashkivenu adoshem*. Was that where it came from? *Hashkivenu* . . . a long time. Yes, that was it. I've been away from you, God. The verse in minor, the chorus in triumphant major. It could be said that the jazz age began with this 1919 song ironically glorifying a mythical Deep South—the Swanee River of Stephen Foster's "Old Folks at Home"—by a pair of New York songwriters who had, as the song's lyricist Irving Caesar quipped, seldom ventured "south of Fourteenth Street," let alone south of the Mason-Dixon line, when they wrote "Swanee." And who better to make it a hit than Jolson, the son of a cantor? A few years ago I saw a revival of *Porgy and Bess* and realized where I had previously heard the musical phrase for the words "it ain't necessarily so." It was at the *bima* on *Shabbos*, when a congregant is summoned to recite a blessing over the Torah. *Borchu es adoshem hamvoroch*. Hear it? I understand from Gershwin's biographer Howard Pollack that "mornin' time and evenin' time" in "Bess, You Is My

Woman Now" comes from the *Ma Nishtanah*, the four questions that the youngest at the Seder asks on the first two nights of Passover, and though I can't independently verify this, I'm prepared to believe that a *Pesach niginah* provided that musical phrase.[14] But that is only one way in which classic American popular song finds its Hippocrene in the Jewish sector of town.

As a lyricist of "Jewish tunes," you needed to modify your melancholy with the wit of insubordination or the gleeful double entendre. You needed cheek as well as cheek-to-cheek, and you needed the ability to sound glad and unhappy at the same time. And of course it didn't hurt if you had a fund of Yiddish words at your disposal. When the chorus in *Animal Crackers* (1930) sings "Hooray for Captain Spaulding, the African Explorer," Groucho Marx, the object of adulation, comments, "Did someone call me *schnorer*?"[15] Nor is a footnote needed when Sammy Cahn writes the phrase "the whole *megillah*" in the title song of the movie version of Neil Simon's first play, *Come Blow Your Horn* (1963).

No one's lyrics sounded more Jewish than Frank Loesser's in select moments in *Guys and Dolls* (1950) and *How to Succeed in Business Without Really Trying* (1961). In the former, there is the moment when Nathan Detroit, more committed to his "permanent floating crap game" than to Miss Adelaide, the burlesque dancer to whom he has been engaged for a record number of years, is on his knees begging her forgiveness for some minor betrayal or other.

> *Alright already, I'm just a nogoodnik.*
> *Alright already, it's true, so nu?*

The incomparable *nu*—which functions somewhat like "well" in English or *alors* in French but with much surplus meaning—is there for the rhyme but not only for the rhyme.[16] It makes these lines impossible to speak or sing without a New York Jewish intonation. Playing Nathan Detroit in the movie, Sinatra never sounded more Jewish.

Sometimes an inversion of customary word order stamps a song as defiantly New York Jewish. "So sue me," Nathan Detroit tells Adelaide. "What can you do me?" In "A Secretary Is Not a Toy," a big playful chorus number in *How to Succeed*, Loesser makes merry with a pun on "pad"—1960s slang for "apartment"—in this couplet:

> *Her pad is to write in*
> *And not spend the night in.*

When, in another big chorus number, the cast sings "company policy is by me okay," it's as though the typically New York Jewish phrasing has become as American as the bagel. But, then, the audience has been prepped. The screwball plot of *Bringing Up Baby* (1938) requires Cary Grant and Katharine Hepburn to sing "I Can't Give You Anything but Love" (music Jimmy McHugh, lyrics Dorothy Fields) to Hepburn's pet leopard, Baby, who is sitting on the roof of the house: "Diamond bracelets Woolworth's doesn't sell, / Baby."

The argument has been made that the Jewish genius—in the sense of a tutelary or attendant "spirit"—is bound up tightly with Jewish wit and humor. You could argue that the most Jewish element of the lyrics written for classic American popular songs is the wit that informs them, whether jubilant or downhearted, buoyantly clever or wryly ironic. Consider Gershwin's couplet in the verse for "Nice Work If You Can Get It":

> *The only work that really brings enjoyment*
> *Is the kind that is for girl and boy meant.*

The inversion of the word order in the second line, which would disqualify it as poetry, accounts for its greatness as a lyric, for it combines the romantic vision of bliss with the spirit of the comic vernacular. The rhyme of "enjoyment" with "and boy meant" is Jewish genius.

The multisyllabic rhyme gives the lyricist the chance to show off his virtuosic powers, as Ira does in retelling Bible stories for "It Ain't Necessarily So." Here in two lines is the crux of the story of Jonah:

> *He made his home in*
> *That fish's abdomen.*

It is hard to outdo Hart in this department. "Mountain Greenery," the pastoral counterpart to "Manhattan," is full of astounding examples:

> *While you love your lover let*
> *Blue skies be your coverlet.*

Leo Robin, in "Diamonds Are a Girl's Best Friend," exemplifies Alexander Pope's definition of true wit as "what oft was thought but ne'er so well expressed." Your average cheating husband will treat a girl all right when the market's up. It's when it crashes that "those louses / Go back to their spouses." There is a decidedly Jewish inflection in Robin's rhyme in "Love Is Just Around the Corner":

> *I'm a sentimental mourner,*
> *And I couldn't be forlorner.*

Hart is peerless at the melancholy of sexual attraction, the masochism of the smitten lover. Given the choice between a quiet, healthy life and the classic quarrel of a man and wife, Hart's lover knows exactly which to prefer. From "I Wish I Were in Love Again," this couplet sums up the whole logic of romance in a noir mode:

> *The words "I'll love you till the day I die,"*
> *The self-deception that believes the lie—*

Sex enters the lyrics sometimes sneakily, sometimes wantonly. Hart rhymed "romance" with the "ants that invaded my pants." Cole Porter uses a geographical conceit that recalls John Donne at his raunchiest. The lover in "All of You" wants to take a tour of his "luscious lass":

> *The eyes, the arms, the mouth of you,*
> *The east, west, north, and the south of you.*

When Porter wrote "Let's Do It," and repeated the word "it" in shifting zoological contexts, everyone knew that "it" was a better euphemism for sex than Walter Winchell's "whoopee" or Dorothy Fields's "digga digga do." Even Irving Berlin gets in on the action in "It's a Lovely Day Today":

A Fine Romance

And whatever you've got to do
I'd be so happy to be doing it with you.

Stairway to Paradise

It may sound like the ultimate paradox, but one distinctively Jewish thing about the authors of the American songbook is the determination to escape from their Jewish origins and join the American adventure. America represented freedom not only from persecution but also from the past, from outmoded rules and obscure regulations, esoteric doctrines and archaic habits of dress. America was an idea, a good idea, even a revolutionary one. You had the freedom to worship and the freedom not to worship, if you so chose. How important it was for Berlin to trumpet his patriotism or for Rodgers and Hammerstein to criticize racism at a time when world Jewry faced the specter of annihilation. The art they made was not an art of defiance—there is little anger or protest in a Rodgers and Hammerstein musical or a Berlin ballad. But in their affirmations of American ideals as they understood them, the writers were pressing back against the forces that aimed to extinguish them.

Oklahoma! opened on March 31, 1943. In that month in Częstochowa, more than one hundred Jewish doctors and their families were rounded up and killed. Ten would die for each of the wicked Haman's sons, who are hanged at the end of the Book of Esther. The Purim month began with a message from the Führer to party members assuring them that his "struggle" (*kampf*) "would culminate with the liquidation of Jewry in Europe." On March 22 at Auschwitz the first of four new crematoria was put to use. On the day *Oklahoma!* opened, Crematorium II made its debut in Auschwitz. It was during that month, too, that my maternal grandparents were deported to Riga. Men in uniforms met them at the station, drove them to the Rumbula Forest, and shot them.

On the surface, *Oklahoma!* took no notice of the war against Germany and Japan, of the atrocities the Nazis inflicted on the Jews, or of the grim Depression that ended only with the coming of war and the boom in the munitions industry. But in an indirect way the show touched upon all these things by offering a redemptive vision, an Oklahoma of the imagination. *Oklahoma!* expressed who "we" were—as Americans and more narrowly as Jews—and what we had to fight for. The show's celebration of cowboy territory seems to reinforce Frederick Jackson Turner's thesis on the importance of the frontier in the American psyche (1893). "To the frontier the American intellect owes its striking characteristics," such as "restless nervous energy," "dominant individualism," and "that buoyancy and exuberance which comes with freedom," Turner argued. *Oklahoma!* bursts with "buoyancy and exuberance," to be sure. But *Oklahoma!* is a love story, and it chronicles the domestication of cowboy territory as if "we" were wedded to the land. In the course of the play, the structural conflict between the farmer and cowman is not only resolved ("Territory folk should all be pals") but resolved in favor of the former: that is, in favor of the forces of civilization. Cowboy Curly, a champion bronco buster, sells his saddle, his horse, his gun belt, and his gun for the sake of farm girl Laurey, and the show closes not only with a wedding but with a celebration of union in a second sense. Oklahoma, still a territory as the show begins, is on the verge of statehood in the first decade of the twentieth century. It will join the Union, and it is just possible that in the logic of displacement favored by Jewish songwriters and librettists, the relation of Oklahoma to the United States as a whole resembles that of the Jewish immigrants to the land that offered them and their kinfolk refuge from the barking nightmares of Europe. As Andrea Most writes in her excellent book, *Making Americans: Jews and the Broadway Musical*, the title song "tapped into wartime nationalism," but the exaltation it releases endures to this day. "The joyous applause that inevitably follows the number joins audience members and performers in the communal utopian vision of Rodgers's and Hammerstein's America," where no one is "better than anyone else." What *Oklahoma!* offered was "a new idea of what America should be—an idea that entailed openness to ethnic outsiders," such as Ali Hakim, the flirtatious peddler, whose Jewish identity is never indicated but can be inferred.[17]

To claustrophobic New Yorkers, beset by wartime shortages and brownouts, here was the American character at its most appealing. The optimism of *Oklahoma!* is the first thing that hits one. There's a bright golden haze on the meadow, and the sky is an endless blue. I have in front of me some of the stamps the U.S. Postal Service has issued in the last few years to celebrate the fifty states in the union. On the thirty-nine-cent stamp representing Oklahoma is the year of the state's admittance to the union, 1907, and next to it, in a bright cursive script, the words "Oh, what a beautiful morning! . . ." Those are Hammerstein's words, from the first lyric he presented to Rodgers. Together (and in collaboration with the choreographer Agnes de Mille and others) they created an idea of Oklahoma to counter the grim reality of the dust storms that caused Okies by the thousands to flee for places west during the 1930s. The exclamatory *Oklahoma!* was an answer to the Oklahoma of *The Grapes of Wrath*, John Steinbeck's novel and, later, John Ford's movie. And the *Oklahoma!* of sunny optimism won out. The land was new and fertile; the country was young and proud of itself. "We know we belong to the land," Hammerstein wrote in the title song, "and the land we belong to is grand." The line recalls the opening of Robert Frost's poem "The Gift Outright," which he read aloud at John F. Kennedy's inauguration but which was first published in 1942, a year before the debut of *Oklahoma!* The poem begins: "The land was ours, before we were the land's." Like Frost's line, Hammerstein's is a statement of manifest destiny, affirming the westward expansion of the American idea from sea to shining sea, white with foam. But both lines also evoke the biblical idea of the Promised Land, and it might be said that Hammerstein's was fueled by two millennia of statelessness. Zionists in Poland were singing the same song with their hands and feet that Hammerstein was voicing in America. It's as though he read the Bible sideways in the manner of the Puritans, transforming Plymouth Rock into Mount Sinai.

In *Oklahoma!* Rodgers achieves the illusion of cowboy music. In the clip-clop rhythms of "The Surrey with the Fringe on Top," he gives so fair an approximation of what cowboy music *might* be like that people listening to the song often assume that it comes from the west of the prairies. They are invariably surprised when they learn that such an *echt* American song was the work of a pair of New York Jews. But the fact is, the "cowboy" rhythms of "The Surrey" sprang entirely from Rodgers's musical imagination—as was also true of "Bali Ha'i" in *South Pacific* and "The March of the Siamese Children" in *The King and I*. Those melodies may sound wonderfully foreign and exotic, but they have nothing whatsoever to do with the indigenous music of Polynesia or Southeast Asia. Rodgers was exercising both his genius and his artistic license. And in proffering a vision of America not as it was but as it might be—not as a fact fixed permanently but as an artistic work-in-progress—Rodgers and Hammerstein were honoring the imperative issued by Ralph Waldo Emerson in his essay "The Poet" (1842). "We have yet no genius in America, with tyrannous eye, who knew the value of our incomparable materials," Emerson wrote. "Our log-rolling, our stumps and their politics, our fisheries, our Negroes and Indians, our boats and our reputations, the wrath of rogues and the pusillanimity of honest men, the northern trade, the southern planting, the western clearing, Oregon and Texas, are yet unsung. Yet America is a poem in our eyes, its ample geography dazzles the imagination, and it will not wait long for meters." *Oklahoma!* fulfilled this prophecy and demonstrated in the process that in singing America's praises, Jewish songwriters were reinventing themselves as American and changing America itself at the same time.[18]

1

My Romance

I love the old folks at home.
IRVING CAESAR, "Swanee"

Jerome Kern and Harold Arlen were my uncles in the synagogue of my boyhood dreams, where I attended services
regularly on Fridays nights and *Shabbos* mornings until I went
away to college. In my mind the music of "Smoke Gets in
Your Eyes" and "Over the Rainbow" was written by Uncle
Jerry and Uncle Harold, respectively, and I felt their invisi
ble presence beside me at choir practice or when we stood up
and praised the "tree of life" on returning the Torah to the
ark. My father was the president of the shul, Congregation
Ohav Shalom (Hebrew for "love the peace"), and as a result
I got to go to many official social functions and sit next to
the honored elders, talkative gents who liked schmoozing
about sports and politics. Hank Greenberg of the Tigers, Sid
Luckman of the Bears, and Benny Leonard of boxing fame
were perennial favorites. Congressman Jacob Javits had a
good reputation for helping get your relatives out of
Yugoslavia. My parents voted to elect him senator even

though he was a Republican and they were FDR Democrats from the moment they set foot in America. In those days when people asked me how I spelled my name, I always said "like the governor" and was understood, though Thomas E. Dewey, Averell Harriman, and now Nelson Rockefeller had succeeded Herbert H. Lehman (no relation) in the governor's mansion in Albany. One thing I like about Ira Gershwin's lyric for Vernon Duke's "I Can't Get Started" is that it mentions "Mr. Lehman—you know, the Gov."

This is the story of a romance, mine, though scarcely mine alone, with an America of the imagination and the primarily Jewish men and women who got to write the book, the lyrics, and the music for the dream. Kern and Arlen and the wordsmiths with whom they collaborated depicted this romance in popular songs that set store by their wit and passion and sophistication. They created, without quite meaning to do so, an art form, and they had a lot of fun doing it. "They Can't Take That Away from Me," "They All Laughed," and "They Didn't Believe Me"—three great songs that begin with the same pronoun—can stand for the many songs that beguiled multitudes, proving themselves in the box office and proving as well that the aims and means of popular culture and high artistic achievement could coincide. The songs of the Gershwins, of Rodgers and Hart, of Irving Berlin, Cole Porter, Frank Loesser, and the rest of a list too long to fit in one sentence retain their power and charm as only true art does. During their effervescent heyday—a roughly fifty-year period between 1914 and 1965—popular songs fed a nexus of other arts and pastimes. The Broadway musical, jazz of the swing and bop eras, Big

Band music and popular vocalists: All depended on the song-writers for their very existence. In a different sense, so did nightclubs and real or make-believe ballrooms. And don't forget the movies that Hollywood turned out in the black-and-white 1940s, when *noir* was new. It's hard to imagine those dialogue-heavy films without "Isn't It Romantic?" or "Body and Soul" (music Johnny Green, lyrics Edward Hey-man), "Baltimore Oriole" (music Hoagy Carmichael, lyrics Paul Francis Webster), or "I Get a Kick Out of You" (Cole Porter) in the background as the plot requires.

Or in the foreground: A marvelous sequence in the 1932 movie *Love Me Tonight* (music Richard Rodgers, lyrics Lorenz Hart) commences when Maurice Chevalier in his tai-lor shop sings a stanza of "Isn't It Romantic?" His customer continues the catchy strain as he walks out the door, where a taxi driver overhears and whistles it, and his passenger, a composer on his way to the train station, takes down the notes, adds words on the train, where a band of soldiers join in, and then the tune becomes a march as the soldiers drill on meadow and hill. Next, a gypsy violinist plays the tune as a melancholy serenade, and finally the princess (Jeanette Mac-Donald) sings a stanza on the balcony of her chateau boudoir. In this Great Depression fantasy, the tailor and the princess are destined to become lovers, you see, despite the vast discrepancy in their social classes, and the song itself is the magic chain that links them.[1]

It was the songbook to which I responded, not the Jewish identity of its authors, though this was a source of pride for me, the son of refugees. Let's put it this way: Every time someone in a movie sings "Hello Mr. Cohen / How's it goin'?" is a minor victory for the Jewish people.[2] To me it remains a source of endless wonderment and speculation that certain Jewish immigrants or their American-born children managed to re-create whole parts of American culture. All right, then. This time the dream's on me. Where or when did it come from? How long has this been going on? Shall we dance? Who stole my heart away? How high the moon? Why was I born?

Fair questions, all, but this being a romance, I need to tell you more about where I'm calling from. Home, where I hang my hat of choice, a fedora, is in the Inwood section of New York City. It's my birthday, June 11, 1956. Bing Crosby recorded Rodgers and Hart's "Mountain Greenery" with Buddy Bregman's orchestra this afternoon. Rodgers is as cheerily melodious as ever, and the lyric is one of Hart's smartest displays of polysyllabic wit. Here's a city boy extolling the "greenery" of God's country by rhyming the word with "beanery," "machinery," and a word formed from the suffix of "cleaner" and the prefix of "retreat." Bing is doing it full justice, I must say. No one sounds more relaxed, even unflappable. In terms that Marshall McLuhan would make fashionable, Crosby is cool and Sinatra is hot. Maybe that's why Sinatra never did as well on television, a notoriously cool medium, as Perry Como did lounging in his sweater—maximum cool. But Sinatra with his high range and Crosby with his deep baritone did harmonize perfectly on a medley of "Among My Souvenirs," "September Song," and "As Time Goes By" on the GE-sponsored Crosby show we saw on TV two years ago. My mother is making wiener schnitzel this evening with cucumber salad and roast potatoes, and my father has promised we will open a bottle of wine and make a special toast. Last night we went to see Hitchcock's latest, *The Man Who Knew Too Much*. I liked James Stewart, my father liked Doris Day, and my mother and my sister liked "Que Sera, Sera," which Day sings in the movie and which I kept hearing all year on the radio, even in the Yankee clubhouse in October. That turned out to be the last time New York fought Brooklyn in the World Series. Well, the Yanks won, Ike was reelected, and inevitably the Ray Evans and Jay Livingston tune copped the Academy Award. Meanwhile, I have choir practice at the temple tomorrow evening. The youth group is meeting next Sunday for a discussion of the function of popular culture during the Great Depression followed by a screening of *Sullivan's Travels*, the Preston Sturges comedy with Joel McCrea as a Hollywood director looking for the real America.

Mr. Birnbaum, a furrier on Dyckman Street in daily life, was the choirmaster of Ohav Shalom. Both he and my father blamed John Foster Dulles for shaming England and France and making Israel give back the Suez Canal to Nasser in 1956. Mr. Birnbaum had a terrible temper. It used to scare me when he gave somebody a piece of his mind until I noticed that every time it happened, his face would turn redder than a Spaldine, the rubber ball we used for games of punchball in the playground, and the veins in his forehead looked as if they would pop. From then on I couldn't take my eyes off him when somebody in choir practice goofed off on his time. I was good at keeping a straight face.

But I liked it best when Mr. Birnbaum talked about Jewish actors he claimed to have known. "I knew John Garfield when he was still Julius Garfinkel," he said. "And the same for Bernie Schwartz and David Kaminsky," who became, as he didn't need to explain, Tony Curtis and Danny Kaye in another space-time coordinate. Sir Laurence Olivier fancied both of these good-looking Jewish boys from Brooklyn, did you know that? No, I didn't. "And don't forget Joey Levitch!" How could I possibly forget Joey Levitch? I remember being eight years old and totally enthralled with this funny-looking, wide-grinning, overgrown kid in a crew cut playing an army chef leading a chorus of GIs in the mess hall singing "Oh the navy gets the gravy and the army gets the beans." And then the sergeant comes in played by Mr. Cool, Dino Crocetti of Steubenville, Ohio, who had become Dean Martin singing "That's Amore" (music Harry Warren, lyrics Jack Brooks) through the same process that turned Joey Levitch into Jerry Lewis, crown prince of Borscht Belt comics. Mr. Birnbaum and his wife had caught Martin and Lewis at the Copacabana in 1949. I'll give you an example of one of their jokes. "Did you take a bath this morning?" "No, is one missing?" Here's another. "Daddy, take me to the zoo." "If the zoo wants you, let them come and get you."

Born in Fürth, not far from Nuremburg in Bavaria, solid and industrious in the German manner, my father ran a small trading firm specializing in the import and export of steel angles, beams, and reinforcing bars. He had an office downtown on Liberty Street, a secretary, and trading partners in places like Belgium and Venezuela, whose postage stamps he brought home for my collection. When I was asked what my father did for a living, I always said, "He's a businessman." My father liked that—just as he liked going to work with a briefcase every day on the subway. But he was a Talmudist to the core, and he loved nothing better than to study the *Gemorah* with like-minded gentlemen, Yeshiva *buchers* from the old country. A devout man who kept the religious law strictly, he tolerated without much of a struggle my widening deviations from the path. After the experience of growing up in Germany, he liked American institutions: West Point, "Hail to the Chief," ice cream sodas, Marilyn Monroe, *South Pacific*, and *Kiss Me, Kate*. He used American idioms as well as he could, calling this fellow "chief" and that one "Mac," but of course his thick Bavarian accent gave him away. I think he winked at the liberties I took because he could see that I, American-born, would have opportunities that would always be denied him, an immigrant with a heart condition, and he didn't want to get in my way. I remember the evenings he lay in his bed listening to Jean Shepherd's radio monologues in the dark. He was also a voracious reader of the *Encyclopedia Britannica*, his favorite purchase. Many a night in my college years I came home late and tiptoed to my room because my father was asleep in his green reclining armchair with the lights on and a volume of the *Britannica* open on his lap to Disraeli's foreign policy or the *Jewish Antiquities* of Flavius Josephus.

Unlike my very serious father, my mother was light-hearted as befit her Viennese girlhood. When with a malapropism she generated laughter, she joined right in. She was an inveterate storyteller and told me many times—in painful detail—about how she escaped from Nazi-annexed Austria to England in 1938 and finally arrived in New York on Thanksgiving of 1939. My mother loved *The King and I*, which we saw at a drive-in, and would sing "Getting to Know You" in the kitchen while preparing dinner. The Rodgers and Hammerstein musical about the King of Siam and the English governess remained her favorite until Alan Jay Lerner and Frederick Loewe came along with their musical based on George Bernard Shaw's *Pygmalion. My Fair Lady* knocked out all competition. On more than one Sunday, the original cast recording with Rex Harrison and Julie Andrews played continuously on our record player. And why not? Even T. S. Eliot loved it. "I must say Bernard Shaw is greatly improved by music," Eliot said. The young Julie Andrews singing "I Could Have Danced All Night" caps the purest expression of joy in a Broadway musical, the triumphant sequence that begins with "The Rain in Spain." For a man with a very uncertain voice, Rex Harrison talked his way through his songs with such artistry it's hard to imagine anyone else doing "Why Can't a Woman Be More Like a Man?" or "I'm an Ordinary Man." When the time came to make the movie version, they replaced Julie Andrews with Audrey Hepburn (and Marni Nixon's voice), but they retained Rex Harrison as Henry Higgins personified. My parents and I saw the movie together when it first came out, and I saw it again, this time dubbed into French, with my friend Jamie in Aix-en-Provence in 1971.

Improbably enough, my mother had met Rex Harrison in 1939 when she worked as a parlor maid in the house of a wealthy London theater producer. One night Rex Harrison came to dinner. "He was very friendly, a real gentleman," my mother said. That was a few months after she had obtained a permit to go to England as a mother's helper. "When I saw how bad the situation was and my parents were still in Vienna, I tried to get them out to England. For America, they had to wait too long, their quota was very small, since my parents were born in Poland." There were sponsors to find, papers to notarize. "Everything took so long, when I finally got everything together England was at war, and my parents couldn't come. I had no way of getting in touch with them."

How often I had heard the story, and how suspenseful it was even though I knew the outcome in advance. "We all received the gas masks and instructions for the air-raid shelters. The American consulate closed, and we had to move to a refugee home. But the American consulate finally opened its doors again, and I received my visa to go to America. How happy I was. Naturally I was worried to travel on an English ship, so my cousin from America sent me additional money, and I changed my ticket to an American ship, the *President Harding.* I think it was the last Atlantic crossing it ever made. It took us ten days of the most terrible shaking. Everyone on board was sick and wanted to die. We were so sick that we weren't even afraid of hidden mines, and as in a dream we did all the safe drillings. The last day was Thanksgiving. We had, and for me it was the first time, a delicious Thanksgiving dinner with turkey and all the trimmings, they played 'Oh, say, can you see,' and when I finally saw the Statue of Liberty, I was really grateful to God, that he let me live and see America."

My father wanted to speak English exclusively and to banish all memory of Germany and the past, and my mother wanted to please him. The reason I speak any German at all was that my parents spoke German when they didn't want my sisters and me to understand what they were saying. My father spoke with a Bavarian accent, my mother with the lighter, more musical accent of her Viennese dialect. One day they had an argument. Each accused the other of speaking English with an accent. They appealed to me to adjudicate. I said that neither of them had an accent. This may sound diplomatic, even gallant, but I heard no accent; I heard the voice of my father and the voice of my mother. Not until years after my father's death, when I heard his voice on tape, did I realize how thick his German accent was when he spoke English.

Some congregants at Ohav Shalom had great stories to tell about how they escaped from the Nazis but didn't want to talk about it except in German among themselves, allowing us kids to tune out and wonder how many points Kenny Sears had scored for the Knicks against Elgin Baylor and the Minneapolis Lakers the night before. I liked basketball well enough, but I liked history more. One person who opened up to me was Mrs. Gottlieb, mother of Joey, who served the best chocolate milk in the neighborhood, using the same syrup they used for egg creams at Nat and Phil's candy store on Sherman Avenue. Joey's mother had been my fourth-grade history teacher in the yeshiva, and I still enjoyed talking about history with her though she had long since retired. I'll never forget the day in August 1964 when she predicted that Lyndon Johnson would win reelection and then escalate the war in Vietnam, belying his self-presentation as a reasonable alternative to Barry Goldwater the hawk. Everyone else at the Democratic National Convention in Atlantic City was singing "Hello, Lyndon" to the tune of "Hello, Dolly," but Mrs. Gottlieb was not impressed. "He's the biggest faker in the United States," she said. It made a big impression, though not nearly so big as the afternoon a few months earlier when she told me about leaving Belgium on foot on May 10, 1940, the day the Germans invaded France and Belgium. She and her husband had owned and operated a thriving jewelry-export business in Antwerp but left everything behind. They were part of a mass exodus, but they didn't panic despite the desperation of their plight. Mrs. Gottlieb felt that keeping a cool head was one of the things that enabled them to survive. They also lucked into an acquaintance with Andree de Jongh, a young Belgian woman their own age who helped many refugees over the Pyrenees and across the Spanish border. "She told us to call her 'Dedee,' which was her code name. It means 'little mother.' But she looked like a schoolgirl. How could this undernourished creature help us? Yet somehow she did. She guided us to Spain and freedom. A true heroine, one of the righteous, it was she who gave us the documents that allowed us to cross the border. You cannot believe how risky this was. And afterward we heard that her own father had been captured and executed by the Nazis, and then the Gestapo caught up with her. They couldn't break her. They sent her to Ravensbrück. She never betrayed a soul. Not a year goes by that we don't write to her on her birthday, November 30. May she live to be ninety."[3] I asked Mrs. Gottlieb for more details, but first she quizzed me on my retention of facts. "What happened on May 10, 1940?" "The Germans marched into Belgium and France, and you and Mr. Gottlieb began your escape." "And what else happened on May 10, 1940?" I shrugged. "Churchill became prime minister," she said. "You have a good head on your shoulders," she told me. She deplored the new trend of ignoring dates and events in favor of analysis of root causes. "They're going to destroy the study of history. A good mind for dates is nothing to sneeze at." It was May 10, 1964. I went to the New York World's Fair a lot that spring and summer. On Broadway Barbra Streisand played Fanny Brice and sang "People" in Jule Styne's new musical *Funny Girl*. On television they were singing, "Wouldn't you really rather have a Buick than any other car this year?"

Erik Schnupp, by day an accountant with a solid civil service job, was nominally in charge of our synagogue's youth group, which meant he scheduled lectures and an occasional movie field trip. The time we went to see *West Side Story*, he denounced it the moment we left the theater, just dismissed it, and then he ostentatiously read an oversized Hebrew book on the long quiet subway ride home. I couldn't stand him. From time to time, however, he brought in a worthwhile speaker, such as the army veteran who came to tell us about his wartime experiences and those of other Jewish men in his company. Karl Frucht had served in a U.S. Army unit composed of European refugees that landed on Utah Beach on D-Day plus one in 1944. In Vienna he had taught history at the university; in New York he worked odd jobs. The army assigned him to a Prisoner of War Interrogation (PWI) team in France and Germany. He explained how odd it felt to be a refugee from a place and to return as a second looey. The Germans had trained thousands of soldiers in English, outfitted them in counterfeit U.S. uniforms, and dropped them by parachute near U.S. lines. This meant (he said) that at checkpoints the PWI officers not only had to do the routine things with extra care—passwords, dog tags—but also had to add methods by which to tell real Americans from Nazi saboteurs. They asked what Sinatra's first name was, who won last year's World Series, and what Broadway musical began with a bright golden haze on the meadow. They never used torture. Never! But they found that even a fanatic Führer-lover would tell you things—important things—if it meant the firing squad rather than hanging at the end of a rope. Some of the "false Americans" were Nazi to the core and stared at them with hatred and contempt. When the boys on the firing squad stood up, their knees shook but at least they had fired a shot for righteousness. They interrogated one man who was personally responsible for the deaths of thousands by lethal injection. The amazing thing was how little his conscience bothered him. Between interrogation sessions he would read Schiller under a blossoming apple tree. One day following the liberation of Paris in August 1944, a PWI captain named Dreyfus stood under the Arc de Triomphe and was wounded when a Nazi prisoner, not properly disarmed, tossed a grenade. To Mr. Frucht that was the meaning of World War II: Captain Dreyfus wins Purple Heart under Arc de Triomphe.[4]

My father's closest friend in shul was Mr. Rosenblatt, a broker at Bache who recommended IBM when people still thought the phone company was a good stock. Mr. Rosenblatt wore first-class Brooks Brothers suits, no vest, spread collars with four-in-hand ties, and cream-colored shirts. He was the most elegantly attired Holocaust survivor in the congregation, with tattooed numbers on his arm to prove it. Bernhard Rosenblatt was seventeen when his family was deported to Auschwitz in 1944. His mother and sister were put to death immediately. His father was killed a few weeks later. Mr. Rosenblatt escaped, survived a death march through the snow, and was blue with typhus when a bunch of GIs rescued him. One of the GIs was the Sutton Place scion of a major brokerage firm. And oh!—look at him now. Bernhard Rosenblatt made his name on Wall Street as an early proponent of index funds. My father asked Mr. Rosenblatt why people should go to a broker for advice if a basket of five hundred stocks tended to outperform an actively managed portfolio? Mr. Rosenblatt smiled and said he had more clients than ever. "Most people want to find a million-dollar baby in a five-and-ten-cent store," he said. "They look at me, and they see a rich man, and when you're rich, they think you really know." My father smiled in appreciation of Mr. Rosenblatt's allusion to *Fiddler on the Roof.* Both men shared a love of Zero Mostel's performance as Tevye, particularly his renditions of "Tradition" and "If I Were a Rich Man."[5] When Mr. Rosenblatt's son Noah and I produced our youth group's variety show, we assigned "Standing on the Corner Watching All the Girls Go By" to ourselves and little Joey Gottlieb. Amy Grossman and I did a duet of "Love and Marriage," and the whole company closed the show with a chorus of "There's No Business Like Show Business."[6]

Of all the congregants in my dream synagogue, my uncles fascinated me the most. From as far back as I can remember,

I knew the words and music to all the songs in Uncle Jerry's *Show Boat* (lyrics Oscar Hammerstein), *Roberta* (lyrics Otto Harbach and Dorothy Fields), and *Swing Time* (lyrics Fields).[7] I loved Uncle Harold's *Wizard of Oz* (lyrics Yip Harburg) from the start, and I had just discovered the jazzy side of Arlen, the Arlen of "Stormy Weather" (lyrics Ted Koehler) and "Blues in the Night" (lyrics Johnny Mercer). Between them, Kern and Arlen represented the two major waves of Jewish immigration to the United States: the first consisting mainly of well-off German Jews, the second and really massive influx consisting of desperately poor Jews from Lithuania and Galicia, the Ukraine, Siberia, and other places in faraway Russia and Poland.

Jerry (born 1885) always had a soft spot in his heart for Harold (born 1905) and put up with all sorts of antics and practical jokes from the younger man. Sometimes when Jerry was playing cards, Harold would come by, wander over to the piano, and complete a Kern tune in manuscript. No one else would have dared do that. Sometimes he razzed Jerry by making a great show of opening the windows to achieve the atmosphere of "tinkling chandeliers" that Kern's music demanded. Jerry had a prized walking stick that once belonged to Jacques Offenbach. This he gave to Harold, who was touched.[8] Mind you, Harold was initially so in awe of Jerry that he called him Mr. Kern for years. When the two of them played golf, Jerry sported jockey caps, captain's caps, or other flamboyant headgear, and Harold wore equally zany shoes. This was in Hollywood, where Kern and Arlen felt right at home: playing cards, golf, sometimes tennis, smoking cigars, driving cars, and going to the track. Not a bad life at all. I have a group photo taken at a black-tie event with a beaming Uncle Jerry standing next to Uncle Harold, his right arm affectionately tucked inside the younger man's left.

II

Tales of the Uncles, Part I

And I brought some corn for popping.
SAMMY CAHN, "Let It Snow, Let It Snow, Let It Snow"

The Start of Something Big

Classic American popular song was the fruit of a revolution that Jerome Kern or Irving Berlin, or both in their individual ways, made happen in two important New York institutions. One was Broadway, the Great White Way, itself as powerful a metonymy for the whole business of show business as its rival across the continent, Hollywood. The other was an undistinguished street in Manhattan's Flatiron district—28th Street between Broadway and Sixth Avenue—which came to be known as Tin Pan Alley. It acquired the name because music publishers had set up their shops there and a cacophony of pianos filled the air. This was during the era just before radios became a fixture of every household's living room. Home entertainment still consisted largely of a piano and voices, and the music industry revolved around the sale of sheet music. News of the new got out through *buskers*, who performed songs for tips in public places the way guitarists today play Beatles songs in the subway, and *pluggers*, who demonstrated the music in the home office or on the road, as traveling sheet-music salesmen. Before 1911, the songwriters of Tin Pan Alley had produced such durable hits as "After the Ball" (Charles K. Harris, 1892), "The Sidewalks of New York" (1894), "In the Good Old Summertime" (1902), George M. Cohan's "Give My Regards to Broadway" (1904), "Take Me Out to the Ball Game" (1908), and "Let Me Call You Sweetheart" (1910). But all that changed in 1911 when Irving Berlin wrote "Alexander's Ragtime Band." Technically, the song was a march, not a rag, and incorporated elements as unusual as a bugle call and a quotation from Stephen Foster's "Swanee River" (1851). But "Alexander" rapidly sold a million copies, made ragtime the rage and Berlin the new "king of ragtime," revived the musical idiom that Scott Joplin had done more than anyone else to establish, and modernized Tin Pan Alley. Berlin's song also launched a new craze for social dancing, since you could dance more easily to ragtime than to the vaudeville ditties or sentimental ballads it displaced.

Though Berlin's mega-hit had all these effects, I hold with those who trace the birth of modern American song to a theatrical event: a ballad Kern wrote for a Broadway show in 1914. August 1914, to be exact—not a slow news month. Let me set the stage. First I shall turn to Benny Carter (alto sax), Oscar Peterson (piano), and Buddy Rich (drums) and play their 1954 recording of Kern's "The Song Is You." Yes, that'll put me in the mood. Just the other day John Ashbery told me that "The Song Is You" (1932) is his favorite Kern song, though this might be explained by his fondness for Guy Maddin's film *The Saddest Music in the World*, in which Kern's melody recurs like a leitmotif. Okay, here goes.

Modern history began when Gavrilo Princip, a young Serbian agent of the Black Hand, assassinated the Archduke Ferdinand, heir to the Austro-Hungarian imperial throne, in Sarajevo on June 28, 1914. There followed tense weeks of negotiations, threats, and all the noise that goes under the heading of "saber-rattling." When the diplomats failed to rein in the runaway horses of imperial armies intent on showing their muscle, Europe galloped giddily into the global conflict that led to the dissolution of empires, the end of royalty, the beginnings of colonial revolt, and a lopsided treaty that virtually guaranteed a reprise of world warfare, not to mention the Russian Revolution and the emergence of the United States, latecomer to the conflict, as a dominant player on the international scene. For more on this epic catastrophe, I recommend Barbara Tuchman's *The Guns of August*. She makes you want to write sentences of epic sweep. For example,

> The Battle of the Marne was one of the decisive battles of the world not because it determined that Germany would ultimately lose or the Allies ultimately win the war but because it determined that the war would go on.[1]

New York was enjoying its isolation from global events when hostilities broke out and war fever swept over the heroic idealists and militant munitions-makers of Europe. On August 24, German troops occupied the city of Namur in

Belgium. On the same day in New York, *The Girl from Utah* opened at the Knickerbocker Theater on Broadway. Like most hits of the time, this musical originated in London and featured a plot as familiar to theater audiences as, in a different register and with different personnel, it would have been to readers of Henry James. The American girl is slated to become a rich Mormon's latest wife, a fate to despise, so she packs up her bags and goes to London to find romance. Serviceable, and the musical did well enough in its West End debut in 1913, but the Broadway producers felt that the first act needed a jolt of tuneful energy. So on that opening night in August the tenor Donald Brian and the soprano Julia Sanderson introduced a new song that the producers had commissioned Jerome Kern to interpolate into the first act.

"They Didn't Believe Me" was short. It consisted of sixteen bars, half the length of the standards to come. The veteran lyricist Michael E. Rourke, who wrote under the name Harold Reynolds, contributed the words, which expressed the singer's joyful disbelief that he (or she) has won the wondrous lass (or lad). It was not the lyric but the melody and its harmonic possibilities that made the song so popular and so influential. "No one had begun writing real songs in this style yet—until suddenly here it was: a perfect loosey-goosey, syncopate-me-if-you-care, a relaxed and smiling American asterisk-jazz song," Wilfrid Sheed writes in *The House That George Built*.[2] Alec Wilder in *American Popular Song* praises the song's melodiousness ("as natural as walking"), noting that it is formally unconventional (consisting of four eight-measure phrases) and "evocative, tender, strong, shapely." David Lloyd George, soon to become prime minister of England, said "They Didn't Believe Me" was the "most haunting and inspiring melody" he had ever heard. George Gershwin heard it on Broadway, decided he wanted to write songs like it, and went to work as a rehearsal pianist for two Kern shows, *Miss 1917* (1917) and *Rock-a-Bye Baby* (1918). The song marked the liberation of its composer from the European operetta tradition (Offenbach in Paris, Strauss in Vienna), and thereby altered the course of both the Broadway musical and the American songbook. Kern, Mel Tormé said, "invented the popular song" when he wrote "They Didn't Believe Me."

The song had an unusual shadow life. So catchy was Kern's melody that a parody version circulated among British soldiers during World War I. Unlikely as it may seem, the lyrics of "War Song" were written by Cole Porter:

> *And when they ask us, how dangerous it was,*
> *Oh, we'll never tell them, no, we'll never tell them:*
> *We spent our pay in some cafe,*
> *And fought wild women night and day,*
> *'Twas the cushiest job we ever had.*
> *And when they ask us, and they're certainly going to ask us,*
> *The reason why we didn't win the Croix de Guerre,*
> *Oh, we'll never tell them, oh, we'll never tell them*
> *There was a front, but damned if we knew where.*[3]

Two million men served on the western front and a great many of them sang this song. You'll hear it if you see the 1969 film version of Joan Littlewood's antiwar satire *Oh! What a Lovely War* (1963). It's the final song on the sound track.

Uncle Jerry

Jerome David Kern was born in New York City on January 27, Mozart's birthday, in 1885, the sixth of seven sons in a solid middle-class family. Having grown up in a musical household, he never seriously considered doing anything else but writing music. This he would do at all hours, phoning friends and collaborators with the results at three or four in the morning if that was when he finished. When did he sleep? When he felt like it, or never. He kept artist's hours all his life. A bon vivant with a sunny outlook, he played poker, bridge, and pinochle, went to the track and bet. He also played golf, mostly on pitch-and-putt courses, and was an avid collector of stamps, coins, old silver, antiques, first editions, and rare books. Though a lousy gambler, he was a shrewd businessman, and he had the temperament to laugh off his losses. He was also a very lucky man away from the card table or casino. Because an alarm clock failed to ring, he did not wake in time to accompany the producer Charles Frohman on an Atlantic crossing departing May 1, 1915. That ship turned out to be the *Lusitania*, which a German submarine sank off the coast of Ireland on May 7, killing more than a thousand people. (Though an early Kern biographer debunked the story, it remains credible.)[4]

Newspapermen thought Kern mildly eccentric. He wore ascot ties. Who wears ascot ties? He was an easy mark. Rare-book dealers would hike their prices if Kern expressed interest in a Shelley first edition or a Tennyson manuscript. He'd pay outrageous sums. The joke was on them in the end, because Jerry's instincts told him to auction his extensive collection of first editions and autograph letters early in 1929, months before the stock market crashed. He netted more than $1.7 million, turning a nice profit at the expense of the same dealers who thought they had fleeced him but were now buying back their wares. With the profits Jerry bought a yacht that he naturally enough called *Show Boat*. So avid a collector was he that a day after he sold his collection he is said to have stopped at a bookstore and bought something that caught his eye, an autograph letter or a first edition containing a note in the author's hand.

Born in Germany, Henry Kern, Jerry's father, prospered in America, operating a merchandising business in Newark. His American-born wife, Fannie, came from a well-to-do family of Austrian Jews. She played piano skillfully enough to have considered a professional career, and it was she who made sure that young Jerome took his piano lessons seriously. From the time he was five, she made him practice, rapping his knuckles with a ruler if he hit a wrong note. Her strictness did nothing to reduce the boy's ardor for improvising on the keyboard. For his tenth birthday, he received the present that changed his life. Either his mother (according to one account) or his father (according to another) took him to see his first Broadway show.

The family lived on East 74th Street. Though his maternal grandfather was the sexton of Temple Emanu-El in New York City, Kern's parents were not observant, and Kern himself married a gentile and lived a thoroughly secular life. In New York, he would go to the Polo Grounds once a week and root for the Giants. He wasn't the most ethnically Jewish young man you've ever met, but at five feet six, bespectacled with curly hair, he was well aware of his Jewish identity. At a poker game somebody made a crack about Jews, and it was Kern, one of several Jews present, who rebuked the anti-Semite.[5] Oscar Hammerstein said he came to Kern with the idea for a musical based on "a story laid in China about an Italian and told by an Irishman." Kern liked it. When Hammerstein wondered what kind of music he would write, Kern replied "it'll be good Jewish music."[6]

At the age of eighteen, Kern was expected to join his father's merchandising business. What happened next illustrated Freud's then-novel notion that our mistakes give us away, big-time: Jerry messed up an order for two pianos and ordered two hundred instead. With his customary good luck, the miscalculation turned into an unlikely commercial success. His father made shrewd use of the installment plan to turn a profit on the two hundred pianos. But the episode persuaded Henry Kern that his son wasn't cut out for business, and he let Jerry attend the New York College of Music and generously financed a year abroad.[7] In Heidelberg, he studied music. In England, he made friends and went to the theater. At the time, British imports dominated the Broadway stage, and Kern wanted to be where the action was. He traveled regularly to London from the time he turned twenty, teamed up with P. G. Wodehouse among other wordsmiths, and grew proficient at writing the kind of songs then in fashion. (It was Wodehouse who wrote most of the lyrics to the show-stopping "Bill" that Kern saved up for *Show Boat*.) Kern became a full-fledged Anglophile. In 1909 he met Eva Leale at the Swan, a pub managed by her father in the village of Walton, where Jerry and two London friends had gone for a holiday. When he heard her practicing scales, he knocked and asked if he could use her piano to work out a melody that had just occurred to him.[8] He and Eva wed a year later. He was twenty-five, she nineteen. After a London honeymoon they settled in New York City. In 1910, a reviewer of Kern's first Broadway show, *Mr. Wix of Wickham*, got it right: "Who is this man Jerome Kern, whose music towers in an Eiffel way above the average primitive hurdy-gurdy accompaniment of our present-day musical comedy?"[9]

Legend has it that Kern caught his first break from producer Charles Frohman only because Frohman thought he was an Englishman and would thus have a native understanding of the London musical stage. In fact, however, Jerry's American accent disclosed his national origins, and his amiable hosts had no trouble placing him on the sociocultural map. George Grossmith, Jr., an actor, lyricist, and innovative producer of West End musicals whose father had made a name for himself performing in Gilbert and Sullivan operettas, befriended the young New York Jew.[10] Grossmith recalled Kern vividly. "Somewhere between the years 1905 and 1910 there was a penniless little Jewish songwriter who hailed from America, but made his home in London. I knew him as Jerry Kern and liked him immensely. He came often to my house and played to us. He played divinely like nearly all of his kind, with a tremendous gift for 'tune.' "[11]

Kern toiled at the songwriter's trade successfully but with no real originality until he broke new ground with

"They Didn't Believe Me." Sinatra sang it on the radio in 1946, soaring as the melody dictates, and Johnny Hartman sang it—and Johnny Mercer and Dinah Shore and Dick Haymes and Julie London. It holds up brilliantly and has everything you want in a romantic ballad. The music climbs from reverent sincerity to the heights of ardor. Perhaps no other popular composer rivals Kern in the ability to reach an operatic climax in a love song. The lyric amounts to several reiterated statements: You're so beautiful (or wonderful), it's incredible, and it's also incredible that you, who could have picked anyone, have picked me. In the lyrics three lines are repeated (four in Sinatra's version). But the music, as William G. Hyland notes in *The Song Is Ended*, "never repeats itself," a major departure from the era of "After the Ball," in which chorus piles on chorus. "It was," Hyland says, "the beginning of that curious Kern blend of European sophistication and American innocence that became his great trademark." It was also Kern's first million-copy sale.

Kern was the link between the Viennese operetta and the modern Broadway show, the creator of "the first truly American theatre music," as Richard Rodgers wrote in *Musical Stages.* In a way, Jerry was everyone's uncle. He had a decisive influence on Rodgers, who was hooked on Broadway from the time he saw Kern's *Very Good Eddie* (1915) when he was thirteen. That event had a greater impact on Rodgers than the bar mitzvah he celebrated that same year (1917): "A large part of one winter most of my allowance was spent for a seat in the balcony listening to *Love o' Mike.*" Kern's music "captivated me and made me a Kern worshiper," Rodgers wrote. "It pointed the way I wanted to be led." Gershwin, too, acknowledged Kern's preeminence. "I followed Kern's work and studied each song he composed. I paid him the tribute of frank imitation, and many things I wrote at this period sounded as though Kern had written them himself."[12]

Life Upon the Wicked Stage

If this were a chronological narrative—the story of the classic American popular song—we would break away from Kern at this point and turn our attention to others who joined him on center stage during the 1920s, the decade that marched in like a roaring lion and gave us much to sing about before exiting like a wounded lamb. George Gershwin wasted no time reaching the heights. Irving Berlin offered him a job as his musical secretary but advised the young man to decline: "You're too talented to be anybody's secretary." George turned twenty-one in 1919, the year he took Tin Pan Alley by storm with "Swanee," which remains to this day his all-time best-selling song. Irving Caesar, who wrote the lyrics, recalled the young Gershwin as a piano virtuoso: "George was a much-sought-after accompanist. They all loved to have George play the new songs. It's like a salesman exposing the inventory. The songs were inventory."[13] George was soon adding to the inventory faster than anyone else. He was the golden boy who could do it all: He could write songs for Al Jolson, then the most popular entertainer in the land, and big orchestral works that fused jazz and the classical tradition. When the clarinet glissando began *Rhapsody in Blue* for the first time in 1924, with Gershwin himself at the piano, it altered the history of modern music and declared the presence of a new hero. That same year he found his ideal writing partner when he and his brother Ira wrote the score for their first Broadway show, *Lady, Be Good!* It was Ira, the Gershwins' sister, Frances, recollected, who "was always the more intellectual one—he's the one who was reading Shakespeare when he was eleven and twelve."[14] To Ira went the daunting task of fitting words to such complex songs as "Fascinating Rhythm" (1924), which the Astaires, Adele and Fred, sang and danced to on Broadway. What followed was an honor roll of classic American popular songs and a musical career unlike anyone else's.

The next to achieve a breakthrough on Broadway were Richard Rodgers and Lorenz Hart, with "Manhattan" in 1925. It was the first in their succession of great hit songs in madly successful Broadway shows. Vincent Youmans teamed up with Irving Caesar, and *No, No, Nanette* contributed "Tea for Two" to the canon of popular songs. Irving Berlin wrote "Blue Skies" as an interpolated song for a Rodgers and Hart musical in 1926, and in Hollywood a year later Al Jolson sat at the piano and sang a jazzy version of Berlin's song to his screen mother in *The Jazz Singer.* The inspired partnership of Walter Donaldson (music) and Gus Kahn (lyrics) produced *Whoopee!* in 1928 with Eddie Cantor introducing "Makin' Whoopee" and Ruth Etting doing the honors for "Love Me or Leave Me." Kern himself turned out "Look for the Silver Lining" (1920, with lyrics by Buddy DeSylva) and "Who" (1925, with lyrics by Oscar Hammerstein and Otto Harbach).

It was with *Show Boat* in 1927 that Kern decisively

advanced the history of the Broadway musical. Kern and Hammerstein broke with precedent when they adapted Edna Ferber's novel for Broadway. What they offered was not a revue, not a bunch of songs linked by some flimsy theatrical pretext, but a play with characters and a coherent plot and with songs appropriate to their changing circumstances. When the show opened, at the end of the year in which Charles Lindbergh flew solo across the Atlantic and Babe Ruth hit sixty home runs, it marked the emergence of the Broadway musical as a popular art form that would generate material for several other art forms (jazz, popular vocals, big band music) and would meet criteria set by drama and music critics on the one hand and by the ticket-paying public on the other. *Show Boat* was the consummate blending of narrative and song, the plot neither fatuous nor absurd, the score full of marvelous tunes that could be abstracted from their dramatic context for dancers to dance to and singers to sing. There are no fewer than five romantic couples in the plot. Two of the relationships fail; spouses desert heartbroken mates. When Julie, the leading lady of the show boat troupe, is revealed to have Negro blood, the consequences are nasty, and neither her marriage nor her vocation can survive the shock of the injustice. This was grown-up stuff—proclaiming love at first sight, vows of eternal fealty, and the efficacy of fantasy, and then proceeding to debunk these very central tenets of the Broadway musical romance. I have seen *Show Boat* performed many times, and I love it the way gangsters in a Brian de Palma movie love Puccini arias. I cry shamelessly. Cotton Blossom, Captain Andy, only make-believe. Fish gotta swim, birds gotta fly. There's an old man called the Mississippi. Life upon the wicked stage ain't ever what a girl supposes. Why do I love you? Because he's just my Bill.

For a composer who thought theatrically, Kern wrote music that lends itself equally to the requirements of opera and jazz. In 1991 the Ambrosian Chorus and London Sinfonietta under the direction of John McGlin recorded "Here Am I," "Bill," "All the Things You Are," "Who?" "Don't Ever Leave Me," "Some Girl Is on Your Mind," and "Why Was I Born?" That all these and other Kern songs received such operatic treatment is not surprising. What is extraordinary is how many Kern tunes have become jazz standards. I spent the afternoon listening to "Smoke Gets in Your Eyes" with trumpeter Clifford Brown, "Yesterdays" with Art Tatum at the piano, "Pick Yourself Up" with George Shearing in Art's place, "The Last Time I Saw Paris" with Bud Powell on the bench, "The Way You Look Tonight" with Roy Eldridge on trumpet and another version performed by Art Blakey and Clifford Brown in New York in 1954, and "Long Ago and Far Away" with Sonny Stitt on alto sax.

Kern hated the words "serious music," because they were always used against him; he thought what he was doing was plenty serious even though it committed the crime of being popular.[15] He might have quoted Poe to good effect: "There are few cases in which mere popularity should be considered a proper test of merit; but the case of song-writing is, I think, one of the few." Kern's popularity was incontestable. Johnny Mercer, who may have been everybody's favorite lyricist, called Kern "everybody's favorite composer."[16] Even purists paid Kern homage. "The task of carrying the operetta beyond the level it has reached in Vienna required a composer American by birth and background, but European-trained, and with sufficient taste to discard the outworn sentimentalities and illusions of both Europe and America (even if only to create new sentimentalities and illusions)," Kurt List wrote. "Temperament, upbringing, and experience made Jerome Kern this composer."[17] A Jerome Kern Jubilee was proclaimed for December 11–17, 1944, and Kern's music was played across the nation. Did the adulation and acclaim go to his head? Let's just say he was an intimidating figure in his later years. Kern liked playing golf with Richard Whiting, who wrote the music to go with Mercer's lyrics for "Too Marvelous for Words." After their tour of the links, Kern would play his latest tunes for Whiting. Four years after Whiting's death in 1938, his daughter Margaret, then eighteen, received a phone call from Jerry inviting her to listen to his new songs and comment on them. "Your father said you were the greatest judge of songs in the business," he told her. She was floored. It was one thing to speak her mind to her father. But Jerome Kern! Luckily for Margaret, herself one of the finest of 1940s singers, the two songs Kern asked her to "judge" were his new collaborations with Mercer, "Dearly Beloved" and "I'm Old Fashioned." Margaret murmured, "Well, what can you say about perfection?" She found one tiny thing that might be changed. "That's very good advice, Margaret," Jerry said. "I'll consider that."[18]

Jerry Kern had great times with "Ockie" (as Oscar Hammerstein II was affectionately known). "Somebody said we were like a pair of truant schoolboys," Jerry recalled with a cold cigar in his mouth. His feelings toward Gershwin were, naturally, more complicated. George had apprenticed for Kern, serving as his rehearsal pianist. In a bantering mood the older composer said, "And here's Gershwin, who showed a lot of promise," and Ira Gershwin, overhearing the remark, wished he had fired back, "And here's Kern, who promised a lot of shows."[19] Jerry wasn't sure how much he liked it that George would, at every party, seat himself at the piano bench as if it were a throne and he the king by universal acclamation and could play as long as he wished though other composers might be present. But no one else played as well as George and it was impossible to stay mad at him. His conceit was accompanied unfailingly by courtesy and charm. When at the age of thirty-eight Gershwin died suddenly of an undiagnosed brain tumor, shocking everyone, Ockie kept the news from Jerry, who was himself recovering from a heart attack. But Jerry figured out what had happened when he turned on the radio that July day in 1937 and all the stations were playing Gershwin songs. And when it was Jerry's turn to go, Ockie gave him a great send-off. He told everyone at the memorial service not to cry because Jerry wouldn't have wanted that. But by the time he had finished the eulogy, he and everyone else were full of tears.

No Field for a Lady

In Hollywood, Kern partnered with the lyricist Dorothy Fields on *Swing Time* (1936), to my mind the most sublime of all the Astaire and Rogers movie musicals, with Irving Berlin's *Top Hat* (1935) coming in a close second. I agree with

Arlene Croce's analysis: "As romance, *Swing Time* is supreme, and stands among the greatest of all screen romances. In no other Astaire-Rogers film is there anything like so exact, so tender, and so magical a sense of the spirit of romantic love that is animated when he dances with her, and that is lost when for one plot reason or another he cannot dance with her. In no other film in the world is dancing used so persuasively as a simulacrum of adult passion and serious sexual commitment."[20] Croce is focusing her praise on the dancing of Fred Astaire and Ginger Rogers, but Kern's infectious melodies and Fields's smart, romantic lyrics, now sassy, now tender, deserve a chunk of the credit. I'm thinking of that moment in "Never Gonna Dance" when Astaire proclaims his indifference to everything around him: "For all I really want is you." From the heights of this assertion in bold iambic tetrameter we move to the comic distribution of items no longer needed by one who has renounced dancing (Groucho Marx will get his cravat and Harpo his "shiny silk hat") before climbing back to the musically sublime mountaintop: "To heaven I give a vow to adore you."

Everyone agrees that Dorothy Fields was the greatest female lyricist, and lest that sound like faint praise, let it be noted that she was inducted into the Songwriters Hall of Fame in 1971, its charter year, in a group of inductees that included Harold Arlen, Leonard Bernstein, Duke Ellington, Ira Gershwin, Yip Harburg, Hoagy Carmichael, Harry Warren, and Johnny Mercer. She was the only woman. An exception in a world of exceptions, Fields had great staying power: She wrote her first Broadway lyrics in 1928 and was still going strong forty-five years later. With her brother Herb she wrote the book for Irving Berlin's *Annie Get Your Gun*. The whole idea for the show originated in Fields's mind when she imagined Ethel Merman, one of her closest friends, in the role of Annie Oakley, belting out songs. "It was the only time in my life an idea came absolutely from God," she said.[21] In the opinion of two other Dorothys—Mrs. Richard Rodgers and Mrs. Oscar Hammerstein—Fields was the most elegant woman of their acquaintance, a superb hostess and onetime heartthrob. At seventeen Richard Rodgers was smitten with Fields, three years his junior, and the two of them could be seen strolling hand in hand in Central Park. Rodgers had met her through her brother Herb, a Columbia buddy, who collaborated closely with Rodgers and Hart in their early years, the trio signing one effort, a melodrama with satirical songs, with a pseudonym composed of their own first names, Herbert Richard Lorenz.

Dorothy and Herb were the precocious children of Lew Fields, a great vaudeville star and later a formidable impresario, the owner of six New York theaters. According to one account, Lew Fields was born Moses Schoenfeld in Poland and came to America with his parents in 1872, when he was five; a second account has Lewis Maurice Schoenfeld born on New York's Lower East Side. He and Joe Weber were the Weber and Fields of turn-of-the-century vaudeville fame. The pair favored broad slapstick custard-pie-in-the-face routines. They also milked their easy-to-affect German-Jewish dialect for all it was worth, and they created at least one immortal punch line: "Who was dat lady I saw you wid last night?" "Dat was no lady. Dat was my wife." Years later, Fields echoed the exchange in countering her father's arguments against her songwriting ambitions. She had her first big gig at the Cotton Club in Harlem, the most risqué and risky of venues, where she teamed up with Jimmy McHugh to write and play the songs sung by black performers to opulent white patrons eager for a thrill. When Lew Fields heard about it, he lost his temper. "The *what* club?" She started to explain, but he interrupted with a tirade against the songwriting profession. That's no field for a lady, he said. And she answered, "I'm not a lady, I'm your daughter."[22]

When Jerome Kern handed her sixteen bars of beautiful music, she aced the audition, returning with "Lovely to Look At." It was the number-one song on the top-ten chart when *Your Hit Parade*, the weekly radio show that chronicled popular taste, made its debut on April 20, 1935. Here and in all her work with Kern she achieves the desired lyricism that the gorgeous melodies require but leaves out the extra teaspoon of sugar. For two of the songs in *Swing Time*—"Pick Yourself Up" and "A Fine Romance"—she wrote the words first and then Kern followed with the music.[23] A reversal of Kern's usual practice, this attests to his respect for Fields's skills— and his willingness to let her lead. If Kern's music in *Swing Time* swings, as it had to do to satisfy the requirements of Fred Astaire, it was probably Fields's lyrics as much as anything else that got him to suspend his operetta impulses and make music for the most talented feet in the land.

"The Way You Look Tonight" won the Academy Award for Fields and Kern, and I would wager that most people with an opinion consider it the best song in *Swing Time*, though I love "A Fine Romance" and "Pick Yourself Up" as much or more. Fields brought out Kern's playful side.

Her lyrics are subtle, inventive, feminine, seductive. When she worked with Kern, he took her with him to the track. Of "The Way You Look Tonight," she said, "The first time Jerry played that melody for me, I went out and started to cry. The release absolutely killed me. I couldn't stop, it was so beautiful." I always liked the story of how she and McHugh came up with "I Can't Give You Anything but Love, Baby." It was what a man said to a woman looking in the window of Tiffany's on Fifth Avenue during the Depression.

Fields combined insouciance and good cheer. Listen to Ella Fitzgerald sing "You Couldn't Be Cuter": "You couldn't be keener / You look so fresh from the cleaner." The brassy Fields, thrusting her hips, can be heard in Peggy Lee's delivery of "Hey, Big Spender": She "doesn't pop her cork" for just any guy she sees. Then there's "I'm in the Mood for Love," the fearless female counterpart to the traditional male carpe diem poem. It's very sexy, and so, in a different way, is "A Fine Romance," one of my favorite love-as-insult songs. I recommend Billie Holiday's jubilant version of 1936, recorded when she was twenty, with Teddy Wilson at the piano and Lester Young on tenor sax. (Billie nicknamed Young "Prez," and he returned the favor, dubbing her "Lady Day.") I get a kick out of the rhymes ("fellow" and "Jell-O"), and the similes make me smile: The male lover is said to be "calmer than the seals in the Arctic Ocean. / At least they flap their fins to express emotion." The impish imagination behind this song is a key to Dorothy Fields's greatness as a lyricist. It's a fine romance that lacks quarrels and is "all morals." Tributes to physical love and the need for two bodies to interlock are seldom delivered with as much awareness of the fine dialectic between attraction and repulsion.

No one had a bad word to say about Fields. She worked with Kern, with Arlen, with Arthur Schwartz and Burton Lane and Cy Coleman. To get an idea of her range, listen to "Don't Blame Me" (Nat King Cole) and then put on "There Must Be Somethin' Better Than Love" (Pearl Bailey). Mel Tormé does a swinging "Pick Yourself Up," the number in *Swing Time* where "peach-melba-voiced Fred Astaire of the feet" (as Frank O'Hara described him) takes dancing lessons from Ginger Rogers, first pretending to be a klutz and then smugly dancing like, well, Fred Astaire. On the same theme, I'm not sure whether to prefer the Sinatra version of "I Won't Dance" ("Ring-a-ding-ding!") or Ella Fitzgerald's playful duet with Louis Armstrong.

I Can't Resist

I can't resist quoting a stanza or two from "An Exuberance, Not a Dump," which May Swenson wrote for her lover in February 1967, because the poet borrows the syntax of one of Dorothy Fields's blue-chip lyrics. Here is how the poem opens:

> *I can't give you anything but sex baby*
> *Creamy waves are washing all the decks baby*
> *Come a while—come with style—you'll come to find*
> *Happy gales, typhoon tails, hurricanes of climax baby*

Sure I'd love to see you making port baby
With some handsome sailor just your sort baby
Till that lucky day here's my report baby
I can't give you anything but sex

And so on, for four more stanzas that glorify the sexual impulse and intimate that it was there all along in the more innocent-sounding accents of "I Can't Give You Anything but Love."

Till the Clouds Roll By

It is January 27, Jerome Kern's birthday. Later tonight I will watch the Kern biopic *Till the Clouds Roll By* (1946), an MGM extravaganza. The movie is diverting in the manner of the 1940s Hollywood homage. It's an airbrushed portrayal of the composer's life, fictionalized at will, with taboo facts cleaned up or transmitted in code—and with a dozen or more glorious song and dance numbers performed by the studio's contract players. Thus, Robert Alda, Alan Alda's father, impersonates George Gershwin in *Rhapsody in Blue* (1945) in which the bachelor's love life is divided between sincere Joan Leslie and sophisticated Alexis Smith, and no one ever says the word "Jew." (The casting of Morris Carnovsky as Gershwin's papa gets the point across.) Cary Grant, tall and raffish, portrays Cole Porter of the delicate features, who neglects his wife Linda (Alexis Smith again) not because he prefers men but because he is married to his work in *Night and Day* (1946). In *Words and Music* (1948)

Mickey Rooney transforms Lorenz Hart into a puckish, cigar-smoking Ariel who gets to sing and dance with Judy Garland. Playing lyricist Gus Kahn, Danny Thomas struggles with self-doubt but is luckily married to decisive Doris Day, who stands by him through thick and thin, in *I'll See You in My Dreams* (1951). The movie may not get its facts straight, but that's entertainment—and besides, it offers by my count more than twenty Kahn songs or snatches thereof, and you can never have a surfeit of "It Had to Be You," so why complain? Each of these movies is worth watching more than once. Each in its way illustrates the process by which Hollywood disguised or masked the ethnic identity or sexual persuasion of its heroes to make them acceptable to a straight public conceived of as a compound of a little old lady in Dubuque; John Q. Public, a CPA, and his wife Jane, who works for the PTA; and Joe Sixpack, a good old boy at a ball game, bowling alley, or bar.

Till the Clouds Roll By ends with a medley of songs in homage to the deceased composer. Not only is Judy Garland on hand playing the Broadway actress Marilyn Miller and singing "Who" and "Look for the Silver Lining," but there's Lena Horne ("Why Was I Born?"), Dinah Shore ("The Last Time I Saw Paris"), the young Angela Lansbury ("How'd You Like to Spoon with Me?"), Kathryn Grayson ("Long Ago and Far Away"), and Tony Martin ("All the Things You Are"). Cyd Charisse and Gower Champion dance ("Smoke Gets in Your Eyes"), Lucille Bremer and Van Johnson sing and dance ("I Won't Dance") and, in a white double-breasted tuxedo and bow tie to match, with as big a band as you can imagine, Frank Sinatra ends the festivities with a sustained crescendo in "Ol' Man River." Critics have pounced on the last in the sequence, and to be sure it's full of incongruity: the rich man's attire for a song about "you and me" who "sweat and strain"; the lean Italian dressed in white singing a song by Jews about the plight of blacks. But this mixing of ethnicities is not a bad thing, and if you can overlook the attire, just listen to the singing. Listen to how Sinatra holds the note between the end of the bridge (where "you land in jail") and the final chorus ("I get weary"). Kern himself, a demanding judge, liked Sinatra's earlier performances of the song, saying, "My idea with that song was to have a rabbity little fellow do it—somebody who made you believe he was tired of livin' and scared of dyin.' That's how you do it, Frankie."[24]

Robert Walker plays Kern in *Till the Clouds Roll By*. A handsome lad who had attended a military academy, Walker, the son of a Salt Lake City newspaper editor, had clean-cut American looks. He had been the young, sweet soldier in *Since You Went Away* (1944), in which Claudette Colbert proves that mother knows best on the home front. In that movie's best-known scene, Walker and Jennifer Jones make the most of the tearful good-bye at the train station that in a World War II movie means the death of the soldier is to come. In biographical fact, Walker and Jones were married at the time and on the verge of a breakup, but from their tear-jerking chemistry on film, you'd never guess that the romance had foundered. Walker plays a soldier again in *The Clock* (1945), arriving in Pennsylvania Station bewildered and naïve and promptly bumping into Judy Garland, who works in an office nearby. The boy's twenty-four-hour leave culminates in an exchange of wedding vows. Such wholesome looks concealed a tragic disposition. After the failure of his marriage, the actor suffered what people used to call a crackup. In 1948 Walker broke out of a psychiatric clinic in Topeka, Kansas, and trashed the local police station after being arrested.[25] He was drunk, drove drunk, and died young, but not before being cast against type and brilliantly bringing to life Bruno Anthony, the crazed and menacing villain of Hitchcock's *Strangers on a Train* in 1950.

As Kern in *Till the Clouds Roll By*, Walker gets to walk along the Mississippi for inspiration, something Kern never got to do in real life. It's an irresistible cinematic moment: The composer walks along the shore of the mighty river, and the opening chords of "Ol' Man River" come to him. Equally fictitious is Kern's senior mentor (a failed composer played by Van Heflin) and his daughter (Lucille Bremer), to whom in turn Jerry becomes a surrogate papa. Much of the drama in the movie has to do with these made-up characters, with just a little left over for Kern's romantic pursuit of his English bride. The movie buries the fact of Kern's Judaism as Kern himself did in life. But sometimes movies in their peripheral details disclose what they are hiding, and that is the case with *Till the Clouds Roll By*. What you need to know about Robert Walker's looks is that on their basis he'd not be denied admittance into the most exclusive WASP country club. Yet throughout the movie, Walker is constantly being mistaken for someone less impressive, someone nebbishy: a piano tuner, a pest exterminator, a hanger-on. At his first meeting with the theater producer Charles Frohman in London, he arrives in the company of other men, and sure enough the producer extends his hand of welcome to the wrong fellow.

Now there are solid grounds for this motif. There is the legend that the producer was so committed to the London model of a musical show that he wouldn't have given Kern a second look if he hadn't thought him English. Also, a climactic moment in the movie's plot, such as it is, is the composition of "They Didn't Believe Me." The film treats the achievement not as the moment when the American popular song came into being but as the defining moment in Kern's emotional life—the triumphant moment when he wins the girl. And the lyric does, after all, suggest an unprepossessing fellow dumbstruck by his good fortune at winning the hand of the girl. Nevertheless, I wonder whether this motif, this notion that the great, the legendary Jerome Kern didn't look like a demigod, was also this MGM movie's acknowledgment of the fact otherwise suppressed in the script: that the man impersonated by Robert Walker, the man behind the hymn to the mighty Mississippi, was in reality a smart Jewish boy with curly hair and horn-rimmed glasses from the city of New York.

In 1945

In 1945, the year Jerome Kern died, the war on both fronts came to a triumphant end. Auschwitz was liberated by Soviet troops, Bergen-Belsen by the British, and Buchenwald and Dachau by the Americans. On April 12 in Warm Springs, Georgia, President Roosevelt said "I've got a terrific headache" and keeled over, dead of a cerebral hemorrhage. Harry Truman didn't even know that we were working on an atomic bomb and were close to success when he was sworn into office. The Russians got to Berlin before we did. The bodies of Hitler and Eva Braun, of Goebbels and his wife, were never found. It was assumed that the Führer had taken his own life after a last vegetarian meal. It took eighty-two days and dreadful carnage for the Americans to defeat the Japanese at Okinawa. On August 9, the second atomic bomb, nicknamed "Fat Man," devastated Nagasaki and demonstrated that the attack on Hiroshima three days earlier was repeatable. When Emperor Hirohito announced Japan's unconditional surrender, he explained that "the war situation has developed not necessarily to Japan's advantage."

On September 9, Sinatra sang "Buy a Piece of the Peace" (music Jule Styne, lyrics Sammy Cahn), urging listeners to buy bonds as they had done "seven times before" in the war years. "There are lands we must police," Cahn wrote. On Broadway, *Carousel* proved that a musical with a tragic plot, including the death of the hero, could please the public. A first-class letter cost three cents to mail. Ballpoint pens came into general use. The GI Bill filled universities across America. Returning veterans had trouble making the adjustment, but the mood was hopeful. Harold Arlen wrote the music and Johnny Mercer the lyrics for a song that encouraged good thinking. The song added several phrases to the language, all imperatives: "accentuate the positive," "eliminate the negative," and "don't mess with Mr. In Between." Of the decade's songs dedicated to positive thinking, and there were many good ones, the best was this, sung by Bing

Crosby and the Andrews Sisters: "Ac-Cent-Tchu-Ate the Positive."[26] When, in the song's release, Jonah and Noah counsel the listener to remain on the plus side of the ledger no matter how dark the circumstances, it is a perfect match of masterly lyric and swinging melody, with enough irony and humor to make the sermon acceptable to optimists and pessimists alike.

The greater irony is that the man who wrote the breezy music for this clever morale booster had, of all the songwriters, the greatest familiarity with the darkest, most desolate corner of the human heart. When I close my eyes I hear him play the piano unseen in a room full of smoke and empty of people except for the bartender and me. It's a quarter to three, and I've been drinking. I could tell you a lot . . . but wait . . . first may I offer this poem in imitation and homage:

"Poem in the Manner of a Hit Song by Harold Arlen
and Johnny Mercer, c. 1945"

You've got to titillate
the body contemplate
the brain and wait
        for the spirit to follow.

You've got to violate
the norms liquidate
the germs and mate
        each girl and her fellow.

Don't hesitate to state
your case, because it's sweet
to be swept off your feet,
        by the handsome stud hero.

It's time to reiterate
the need to celebrate
and not be celibate
        so you don't die solo.

III

Tales of the Uncles, Part II

O.K. by me in America!

STEPHEN SONDHEIM, "America"

Uncle Harold

Uncle Harold's real name was Hyman (or Chaim) Arluck (or Arluch). He was born in Buffalo, New York, in 1905, and his father was the longtime cantor of Temple Adath Yeshurun in Syracuse. Samuel and Celia Arluck always called their son by his Hebrew name, Chaim. He had a twin brother, who died the day after their birth. From the age of seven, Chaim sang in the choir and listened in awe to his father's improvisations on old liturgical chants. Cantor and Mrs. Arluck spoke in Yiddish and observed strict orthodox laws. Still, Hyman's Yiddish-speaking pop deviated from the stereotype of the stern, disapproving, and even uncomprehending old-world cantor perpetuated by *The Jazz Singer*. Not only did Shmuel Arluck tolerate his son's defection from the orthodox camp but—so proud was he of the young man's musical accomplishments—he would adapt the Saturday prayer services in shul to the songs written by his son. According to accounts I have read, the songs he favored for Sabbath services included "Over the Rainbow" and "Come Rain or Come Shine." I sometimes wonder if, when dancing with the Torah—or perhaps on Purim—he ever chanted to the tune of "Ding, Dong, the Witch Is Dead."

Like Gershwin, Arlen was hooked on jazz and the blues. "A lot of George Gershwin rubbed off on Harold," said Yip Harburg. "George was Harold's deity, he really was. George brought to American music a combination of his own Semitic background and melded it to the Negro jazz." In conversation with Max Wilk, whose book of interviews with the songwriters (*They're Playing Our Song*) is a fantastic source of anecdote and information, Yip pointed out that Harold was as temperamentally different from George as two men can be. "Harold is a very, very melancholy person. Inside, deeply religious. But he's very superstitious. When he gets to the piano, it's a feeling of witchcraft. He'll spit three times and almost talk to the chords, talk to God. He'll do it humorously, but behind the humor are all sorts of superstitions and beliefs." Harold sang and played the piano—in nightclubs—before he realized that he could compose music. "I was jazz crazy," he told Max Wilk. "I don't know how the hell to explain it—except I hear in jazz and in gospel my father singing. He was one of the greatest *improvisers* I've ever heard." Harold brought home a recording of Louis Armstrong, and there was a hot lick in there, and his father gave him a stunned look of recognition. "I can remember improvisations of my father's that are just like

Louis Armstrong's—and, remember, my father came from Eastern Europe when he was eleven years old."[1]

As a young man Arlen thought of himself as a pianist and singer. He sang with his father in temple on the High Holy Days, but by the time he was fifteen he was hooked on jazz and the blues. His first job was playing piano for a vaudeville trio. He also played for silent-movie theaters in the Buffalo area. He quickly realized that he had to get out of Buffalo. "To commit suicide in Buffalo would be redundant," he said.[2]

Where else to go but New York City? In Manhattan he roomed with Ray Bolger, the dancer who went on to play the Scarecrow in *The Wizard of Oz*. Bolger recalled "the wistful feeling in anything he did, in his conversation, when he mentioned his father, or talked about what he was going to do. His ambition, however, was not a driving force, but something very sympathetic and sweet. And his wonderful sense of humor—it was never an insult kind of humor, but a teasing kind."[3]

Harold had his big breakthrough with "Get Happy," which began as a vamp. Harry Warren, who went on to compose such hit songs as "Chattanooga Choo-Choo" and "There Will Never Be Another You" (both with lyrics by Mack Gordon), heard it and encouraged Arlen to turn the riff into a song. Warren said he knew just the right man to write the words: Ted Koehler. Warren was right. Arlen and Koehler were a natural team. They succeeded Jimmy McHugh and Dorothy Fields at the Cotton Club, where they turned out two shows a year from 1930 to 1934. The fellows made fifty dollars a week plus sandwiches and absorbed more than just the ambience of the legendary club where Duke Ellington and Cab Calloway performed. If Arlen's music is jazzier than that of just about any of the other popular songwriters, this reflects his discovery of jazz at the age of fifteen—his ticket to freedom from Buffalo and the world of his parents—and the early influence of Gershwin, whose "Swanee" made a huge impression on Arlen in 1919. But surely the time he spent at the Cotton Club had something to do with it as well.

In his New York years Arlen read Rilke, Montaigne, Nietzsche, Marcus Aurelius. He carried a notebook with him wherever he went in case the kernel of a melody occurred to him. When, in the 1930s, Hollywood beckoned, Arlen joined the other composers (Kern, Berlin, Rodgers), who went west. He fit right in, playing tennis and golf, especially golf, and making home movies of the Gershwin brothers, Al Jolson, Dorothy Fields, and Judy Garland and the cast of *The Wizard of Oz*. While he was driving on Sunset Boulevard, the first bars of "Over the Rainbow" came to him. He and Yip Harburg, "the Yipper" as Harold called him, had completed what they called the "lemon-drop songs" for *The Wizard of Oz*. Now they needed a big ballad. The deadline neared. Arlen grew anxious. The tune popped into his head as the car passed Schwab's drugstore. "It was as if the Lord said, 'Well, here it is, now stop worrying about it!' "[4]

Arlen's songs were more complex and unconventional than anyone else's. George Gershwin, who admired Arlen and befriended him, once asked him, "Harold, why do you get so complicated? People can't sing these songs."[5] Arlen stretched the conventions of the thirty-two-bar form. This made him a favorite of the other composers. But it also helps to explain why he was, despite the tremendous success of *The Wizard of Oz*, less famous than he deserved to be. He never enjoyed the success on Broadway that Kern, Berlin, Porter, Gershwin, and Rodgers all achieved. People whistled "Stormy Weather" or "Paper Moon" and if you asked them who wrote that song, they'd say Berlin or Porter or Rodgers, and if you told them it was Arlen, they'd say "Who?"[6] The darkness in some of Arlen's songs may be attributable, as Wilfrid Sheed argues, to a case of latent depression that grows to the point that one can no longer distinguish desire from despair. But it also implies a musical affinity with the blues (nicely defined by Sheed as "spirituals with a hangover").[7] With Ted Koehler, Arlen wrote "Ill Wind." With Johnny Mercer, "Blues in the Night." With Yip Harburg, "Last Night When We Were Young." Ethel Waters, who sang Arlen's songs when both worked at the Cotton Club, said that Arlen was the "Negro-est" white man she knew.[8] He had a right to sing the blues. According to Sheed, Arlen's father may have chanted the liturgy to his son's songs, but Harold's parents never quite forgave him for marrying Anya, a *shikse*—a showgirl yet—and one with a precarious grip on her sanity; Anya eventually had to be institutionalized. "Arlen could do no wrong in the 1930s and nothing right in the 1950s," Sheed writes. When Anya died of a brain tumor in the sanatorium in 1971, Arlen could "feel like a bad son, a failed husband, and a burned-out songwriter all in one go."[9] After Anya's death, he withdrew entirely and spent the last fifteen years of his life in a state of black depression, unable to work, a confirmed recluse except for his daily telephone

conversations with—and annual birthday poems from—
Irving Berlin. Irving had a big heart.

A Brief Digression on Irving Berlin

When asked to define Irving Berlin's place in American
music, Jerome Kern replied, "Irving Berlin has no 'place' in
American music. Irving Berlin *is* American music." It's a
great line that everyone quotes in the same way that everyone quotes Dean Martin on Sinatra ("It's Frank's world. We
just live in it."). But, then, Berlin inspired superlatives. In
George Gershwin's opinion, Berlin was "the greatest songwriter who has ever lived," America's answer to Franz
Schubert.[10] And if your idea of Berlin is limited to the
anthems he wrote—"God Bless America," "White Christmas," "Easter Parade," "There's No Business Like Show
Business"—well, there's that side of his genius, sure. But he
also wrote songs that swing. Listen to the Berlin songbook
that Ella Fitzgerald recorded in March 1956 with arrangements by Paul Weston. Yes, he wrote songs of simple sincerity and sentiment: Let's have another cup of coffee. Let's
take an old-fashioned walk. It's a lovely day today. But if it's
wit you want, Berlin will give you a sultry beauty capable
of starting a heat wave by "letting her seat wave." Berlin
can be sweet and sly at the same time. I think of the little
ruse proposed—presumably by telepathy—by the suitor in
"Change Partners": Tell the guy who's monopolizing your
evening that you want to sit out the next dance, then "I'll
tell the waiter to tell him he's wanted on the telephone,"

and then you can dance with me. Berlin wrote great songs for dancers in general and for Astaire and Rogers in particular: "No Strings (I'm Fancy Free)"; "Puttin' on the Ritz"; "Top Hat, White Tie, and Tails"; "Cheek to Cheek"; "The Piccolino."[11]

Berlin wrote the comic songs in *Annie Get Your Gun*, an array of weather songs ("Heat Wave" for summer, "I've Got My Love to Keep Me Warm" for December, and "Isn't This a Lovely Day" for any old rainy day), love songs ("How Deep Is the Ocean?"), shouts of joy ("I Got the Sun in the Morning"), and ballads ("What'll I Do?"), amid lesser-known tunes as flat-out charming and stylistically unlike one another as "Soft Lights and Sweet Music" (listen to Lee Wiley's version) and "Be Careful, It's My Heart" (Tommy Dorsey's band, vocals by the young Sinatra). For Alec Wilder in *American Popular Song* (1972), Berlin was simply "the best all-around, over-all song writer America has ever had." Others may have surpassed him in one area or another, and he himself was inept at the piano, but only he mastered "the entire range of popular song." Wilder, who usually had no trouble summing up a composer's signature style, confessed himself incapable of defining Berlin's, because Berlin was so fluent and so various and could go with astonishing ease from the urbane elegance of Astaire and Rogers in *Top Hat* to the bucolic bumptiousness of Ethel Merman singing the lead in *Annie Get Your Gun*.

Jerome Kern had signed on to write the score for *Annie Get Your Gun*. Dorothy Fields would write the lyrics, and she and her brother Herbert would provide the book. When Kern dropped dead on a New York City street, the producers—who happened to be Richard Rodgers and Oscar Hammerstein—asked Berlin to take over. He did, and in record time he created one of the great scores in Broadway history: "There's No Business Like Show Business," "You Can't Get a Man with a Gun," "I Got the Sun in the Morning," "Doin' What Comes Natur'lly." (The critics weren't as impressed as you'd think they'd have been, but that's a familiar story.) Because Berlin wrote the words for his own songs, Fields was relieved of her responsibility for the lyrics. She was typically gracious, making no fuss, and Berlin typically generous, increasing the size of the take that went to the Fieldses at his own expense.[12] One day the producers asked Irving about a big chorus number he had played for them, which seemed to have disappeared. He said he had dropped it. Why? Because he assumed they didn't like it. What gave him that idea? They had not said anything when he played it for them. That was, Rodgers hastened to explain, because he and Hammerstein were speechless with admiration when they first heard "There's No Business Like Show Business." When inspired, Irving was almost as fast a composer as Rodgers and less defensive about it. He wrote the great "contest song"—the one that begins "Anything you can do I can do better"—in a taxicab following the Saturday meeting in which it was decided that *Annie* needed one more song even though rehearsals were set to begin on Monday.

Born Israel (Izzy) Baline, Berlin had come to America at the age of four from Mogilev in eastern Belarus, or possibly from a godforsaken village in Siberia, where the locals needed no excuse to beat up the Jews. Moses Baline, a *chazzan* like his father and grandfather before him, took his wife and eight children to America and settled the family in three crowded rooms without windows on the Lower East Side of New York. In the local synagogue Izzy sang with his father, but the old man died when the boy was eight, and he promptly dropped out of school, sold newspapers in the streets, and learned his trade as a busker and a plugger. Though Berlin's cantor father had made ends meet as a kosher poultry inspector, his son was as *treyf* as the fare in the Chinatown restaurant, the Pelham Café, where he earned his bucks as a singing waiter. He could play piano in only one key, that of F sharp—he had taught himself to play piano using the black keys only. Though he needed assistants to write out the notes of the songs he composed, he managed to write thirty Broadway shows, seventeen movie musicals, and nearly three thousand songs. Despite the occasional speedy burst of brillance in the back of a cab, he didn't make it look easy. One observer said that watching Berlin work on a song was like watching a woman in labor.[13] He couldn't sing very well, and his appearance was not prepossessing. Yet when he took the stage in an army uniform and sang about how he hated to wake up in the morning and would like to strangle the bugler, he became as American an icon as James Cagney playing George M. Cohan marching and singing "Over There" at the end of *Yankee Doodle Dandy*.

In "You're the Top," Cole Porter singles out the "Berlin ballad"—"Always," "How About Me," "How Deep Is the Ocean?"—as best in class. (Others have said the same of the "Rodgers waltz.") And Berlin repaid the compliment, writing several raunchy stanzas in a send-up of "You're the Top" that people assumed Porter himself had written until

Robert Kimball's *The Complete Lyrics of Cole Porter* set us straight. In Berlin's version, "you" are not only the "burning heat of a bridal suite in use," but also the bosom of Venus, "King Kong's penis," and "self-abuse."

Doesn't that sound like Porter, only more so?[14] Only after Robert Kimball showed me the parody lyric did I realize that Berlin was to Porter what Kern was to Rodgers: the model, the inspiration, the influence. Certainly Berlin gave Porter some of the best advice he ever got: "Never apologize for a song that sells a million copies."[15]

Next to Arlen, Berlin had the most Jewish background of the major songwriters, yet it was he who went the furthest in assimilating to American social norms. Though he started as a Democrat, he ended as a Republican, and it was he who minted the greatest campaign slogan in American presidential politics: "I Like Ike." In the 1920s Berlin was at the center of a big scandal because he wooed and wed not just any gentile goddess but Ellin Mackay, the heiress to a fortune, from a strict Roman Catholic family. Ellin's father, himself a hapless heir unequal to the task of managing the family's telegraph empire, threatened to disown her if she married the cantor's son. She did, and Clarence Mackay made good on his threat. But the lovers had their way, and by all accounts it was a very loving marriage. Yet I can't have been the only one not surprised to read in Mary Ellin Barrett's affecting memoir of her parents that Irving and Ellin "had their first bad fight" over religion. As Barrett writes, "My parents might be nonbelievers and have put my religious upbringing on hold." Nevertheless, "they might have had their first bad fight when my mother suggested raising me as a Catholic, such a terrible fight, she would say later, such rage on both sides, that she did not ask again."[16]

As things worked out, the improvident tycoon lost his money in the crash of '29, but Irving Berlin's songwriting talent provided handsomely for his family, and mutual forgiveness may have been achieved when Irving gave his old tormentor a million dollars in the dire days of the deep Depression. Money! One of my favorite Berlin couplets combines love and lucre: "I've got a great big amount / Saved up in my love account." That's from a song that Ella Fitzgerald and Louis Armstrong began singing when I commenced writing this paragraph. The song is "I'm Putting All My Eggs in One Basket"—exactly what you're told *not* to do with your investments. The use of this hoary adage as the trigger of a song arguing against what financial analysts term "diversification" in romance perfectly exemplifies Berlin's virtues of simplicity and the common touch. One of Berlin's nine fundamental rules for songwriting was, "Make the song as simple as possible."

Time, which had put George Gershwin on its cover in 1925, granted Berlin the same honor in May 1934, with a portrait of the composer in concentration at the piano. But by 1919 Berlin had already formulated the key rule for songwriting as not only an art but a profession: "The song writer must look upon his work as a business, and that is, to make a success of it, he must work and *work*, and then WORK." Toward the end of his very long life—he died at the age of 101 in 1989—he soured on what had happened to pop culture. Still, he had to admit that he hadn't done badly "for a poor immigrant boy who can't read music." Oh, I could spend the rest of the afternoon regaling you with Berlin stories and tunes.

Uncle Harold (continued)

Some think Uncle Harold was the most talented and innovative of all the songwriters. Steven Blier, the artistic director of the New York Festival of Song, calls Arlen the "mystic" who "brought some of the ecstatic transport of religious worship to the popular song." The "spiritual" element, in several senses, is strong in "Get Happy" and "Ac-Cent-Tchu-Ate the Positive." Arlen would let the music lead him and to hell with people's expectations. Not a phrase is repeated in the first eight bars of "Stormy Weather," while in "Come Rain or Come Shine" the melody consists largely of a single repeated note—it's the harmony that creates the song's richness of affect.[17]

Among the most passionate of Arlen's fans was Alec Wilder. Wilder said that Arlen was the protégé who outdid his master, Gershwin. Wilder has a lot of opinions. He thinks Cole Porter overrated: "Overall, I find Rodgers warmer, Arlen more hip, Gershwin more direct, Vernon Duke more touchable, Berlin more theatrical." Wilder thinks Rodgers declined into "musical complacency" almost from the moment Hammerstein replaced Hart on the ticket, and he is unafraid to dissent from the majority view of "Some Enchanted Evening": "I'm in church and it's the wrong hymnal." But you need not share Wilder's opinions to recognize in him—the composer of "I'll Be Around"—the precise admixture of authority, conviction, and independence of mind that makes for a great guide. He is certainly right to put "You're the Top" at the top of all Porter's "list" songs, and the competition is stiff. He may evince heresy in judging Gershwin as not "in the same league as Jerome Kern or Richard Rodgers as a pure melodist." Still, it is not his judgment but the complexity of his response that makes it so valuable. Consider: "[Gershwin] was an aggressive writer. He was the 'hard sell,' as opposed to the softer, gentler persuasiveness of, say, Kern or Irving Berlin. If I were to compare his songs with Kern's, I'd say Gershwin's were active and Kern's passive. The constant, and characteristic, repeated note found throughout Gershwin's songs is a basic attestation of this aggressiveness." Again: "It's truly extraordinary how constant is Gershwin's use of repeated notes." Or: "The verse to 'Nice Work If You Can Get It' is especially fine, with an expert triplet unexpectedly showing up in the middle of the fourth measure, unrepeated at any point." It meant something that Wilder, whose love of popular song makes him so demanding a critic, says that with Arlen he has to "guard against over-enthusiasm. For just at the time I started to try to write songs, I came upon his own early published music. I had listened to Jerome Kern, in particular, as well as Vincent Youmans, George Gershwin, and early Richard Rodgers, but something resembling an electric shock occurred when I first heard Arlen's 'Sweet and Hot' (1930). This shock has been repeated many times in the many years since."[18]

Uncle Harold took me aside one October day and said he would introduce me to three of his collaborators. Yip Harburg was easy to approach. Born Isidore Hochberg to orthodox Jewish immigrants in 1898, the Yipper wrote, in addition to *The Wizard of Oz*, the lyrics of "April in Paris" (though he had never spent a day in *la ville lumière*), and the Burton Lane songs in *Finian's Rainbow* ("That Old Devil Moon," "When I'm Not Near the Girl I Love"). He became a political radical in the 1930s and held his convictions with religious fervor. In 1932 Yip wrote the words for "Brother, Can You Spare a Dime?" (music by Jay Gorney). Fifty million people heard the young Bing Crosby put an Irish face on this Jewish ballad of the American working man.

With Arlen, Harburg wrote "It's Only a Paper Moon" and "Last Night When We Were Young." (There are many wonderful versions of the former, but Alec Wilder is right about "Last Night." Once you hear Sinatra's 1954 recording, there is no other.) An Arlen-Harburg song with the buoyancy that only fast internal rhyming can give you is "Lydia the Tattooed Lady," written for the Marx Brothers movie *At the Circus* (1939). Harburg rhymes "Lydia" with "encyclopiddia" and tells us that the lady "has eyes that folks adore so / And a torso even more so."

Like so many of the boys, Harburg came from the Lower East Side. He went to Townsend Harris High School with Ira Gershwin, wrote light verse for the school paper after school, and worked nights lighting streetlamps for three dollars a week plus change. Gershwin invited Harburg to visit his house and played Gilbert and Sullivan's *HMS Pinafore* on the Victrola. "I was starry eyed for days," Yip said. For the school newspaper he and "Gersh" wrote a column they called "Much Ado." In 1914 the fellows went on to the City College of New York (CCNY), that hotbed of smart Jewish kids, and revived the column (now called "Gargoyle Gargles") for the campus newspaper.[19] The light verse that Harburg and Gershwin wrote collaboratively in college proved the ideal apprenticeship for a career as a lyricist. With an assist from Gershwin (who contributed the verse beginning "When all the world is a hopeless jumble," not sung in the movie), Harburg wrote the words for "Over the Rainbow." That greatest of Arlen melodies had to overcome a number of obstacles on its way to becoming Judy Garland's anthem of Oz. When Arlen played the music for Harburg, the lyricist was not impressed ("That's for Nelson Eddy, not a little girl in Kansas") and the two agreed to play it for Ira and let him serve as arbiter. Luckily, Ira liked what he heard, and so lyrics were added to the melody. Amazingly, the song was deleted three times before the halfhearted heads of MGM let it stay in the movie.[20]

A second Arlen lyricist I met is someone everyone in the business loved and cherished, Johnny Mercer, whom I think of without fail when walking on Mercer Street, a few blocks from where I live in Greenwich Village, just as I think of Bing on Crosby Street a few blocks farther east. (I also treasure misprints of Arden Street, the street I grew up on. It was Auden Street on a first-day cover in 1958, and I still have the envelope that reached me on Arlen Street around the time of Judy Garland's 1961 concert at Carnegie Hall.)* Genial Johnny sang beautifully. It's his voice you hear on the

---

* A first-day cover is an envelope with a postage stamp canceled on its first day of issue. Many first-day covers contain decorative elements and become collectibles.

sound track of *L.A. Confidential* singing "Ac-Cent-Tchu-Ate the Positive." Mercer wanted a song to say "I love you," or whatever it had to say, in words that a guy on a bar stool could appreciate. He had a weakness for the phrase "rain or shine" the way the Gershwins liked "who could ask for anything more?"[21] Variants occur in "Dearly Beloved" and "Day In, Day Out." The best example, written with Arlen, is "Come Rain or Come Shine." Arlen gave Mercer the music and the latter instantly came up with the song's opening line: "I'm gonna love you, like nobody's loved you." Mercer was stuck until Harold added, jokingly, "come hell or high water." "Of course," Mercer said. "Why didn't I think of that . . . come rain or come shine."

With its unsettled tonality, going back and forth between major and minor keys, and its emphatic use of repeated notes, Arlen's music for "Come Rain or Come Shine" virtually obliges Mercer to write a "Jewish lyric"—to write against the grain of his assertions. This musically demanding song makes "I love you" sound real though shot through with anxiety: There is resolve here, and sincerity, and even some of the hyperbole we expect in a love song (where mountains measure height and rivers depth), but there is little euphoria or jubilation. What is affirmed is a love greater than circumstance, and what it implies is that circumstances don't look too good. The song offers a quotation from Cole Porter. When we started our romance we thought "it was just one of those things." But—the song keeps saying "but"—*this* is for always. There is skepticism to overcome, and consequently there is equivocation here as well as affirmation. Mercer's doubt-sowing words, "We're in or we're out of the money," are unusual in a love song, especially if you grant that "money" stands for something besides money. The phrase is a radical revision of Al Dubin's lyric for "We're in the Money" (music Harry Warren), which Ginger Rogers sings giddily in pig latin among Busby Berkeley's dancers at the start of *Gold Diggers of 1933.* "We're in the Money" was exuberant, a pure example of art as a species of wishful thinking. We're not going to be afraid of the landlord anymore. No, we're going to look that guy right in the eye. The Depression was a feeble old man who done us wrong but is through. That was in 1933 when the United States had a new president who advocated fearlessness but the economic crisis was still acute. Mercer and Arlen wrote "Come Rain or Come Shine" in 1946: The Depression was behind us for real this time, we had emerged triumphant on both fronts in World War II, and it was all right to communicate ambiguity and foreboding in a love song.

Mercer was not Jewish, but I like to think of him as an honorary Jew. After all, he wrote the lyrics for Ziggy Elman's "And the Angels Sing," which is either the jazziest klezmer tune or the most Yiddish swing song. It's magic: In my mind the names Mercer and Arlen merge until what is left is Merlin. The two of them got along swell. They used to drive around and talk. Usually what happened is that Harold would play the song and John would listen, make some mental notes, and then leave. When he returned, he had the lyric in hand. This was before they had tape recorders. What recall Mercer had! And he could produce verbal complexities to rival the musical ones of his partner. "That Old Black Magic," a superb piece of music, longer than the customary thirty-two bars and more intricate, has a lyric that fits it perfectly, with a couplet at its core that the groom might recite to the bride on their wedding day: "For you're the lover I have waited for, / The mate that fate had me created for." The exquisite multisyllabic end-rhymes ("waited for / created for") reinforce the internal rhyme of "mate" and "fate" and lead to the kiss that captures the lover's heart. It is that rare song that conveys all the romantic enchantment of falling passionately in love at the same time that it hints at the tyrannical nature of Eros. I still remember the first time I heard it: I was nine years old and sitting in the movies, waiting for the feature, when a short came on with Louis Prima and Keely Smith doing "That Old Black Magic." Years later I learned from a respected biographer of Mercer that Johnny had had a tempestuous affair with Judy Garland and that he may have been thinking of her and her predilection for oral sex when, in "That Old Black Magic," he likens the experience of love to riding an elevator going down and down—a piece of information that lodges in your head once you hear it, though happily without detriment to the song."

Everyone knew that John drank too much and was a nasty drunk, and perhaps only a gentlemanly drunkard with a dark side and a lousy marriage could have written "One for My Baby, and One More for the Road," which Astaire introduced and Sinatra made famous. Go over the lyric and you'll see that few specifics are given about the "brief episode" that has ended. All is innuendo and implication. In memory, the song is about the end of a love affair. But the text is really something else: It's a drunken loser's self-praising and somewhat incoherent lament. The song even refers artfully to itself: "I've got the routine. Put another nickel in the machine." Not only the nickel of those pre-inflation days but the jukebox itself, now living only in memory, reminds us how much time has passed since Arlen and Mercer collaborated on this song. They also came up with "My Shining Hour" (I recommend Mabel Mercer's version) and "Blues in the Night." The latter was up for an Academy Award but lost to "The Last Time I Saw Paris" by Kern and Hammerstein. "You should have won," the winners told Arlen and Mercer. "You had the better song." It's true. As someone joked, it was the only time an Oscar had been stolen by an Oscar.

Harold's first collaborator was the seriously undervalued Ted Koehler (1894–1973). "Get Happy" is a hybrid of jazz and spiritual, a hallelujah chorus evoking the exodus of the children of Israel from Egypt: "We're going to the Promised Land." Yip Harburg said that Arlen fused the impulses of Hebrew and black music to come up with something distinctively American, and this may be truest of the songs he wrote with Koehler. The two men wrote "Between the Devil and the Deep Blue Sea" (1931), "I've Got the World on a String" (1932) and "Stormy Weather" (1933) for the Cotton Club. The pair also wrote "I Gotta Right to Sing the Blues" for a Broadway show in 1932 and "Let's Fall in Love" in Hollywood a year later for a movie. "Stormy Weather," a breakout hit for Ethel Waters and Lena Horne, stands at the dark end of the spectrum, "gloom and misery everywhere." At the opposite end is the exuberance of "I've Got the World on a String." In 1953 Frank Sinatra kicked off his Capitol years, probably his finest period, with "I've Got the World on a String." Few of Arlen's songs sound so happy. The singer has it in his power to sit "on a rainbow" and "make the rain go." The felicitous internal rhyme of "string" and "finger" in Koehler's lyric corresponds exactly to the syncopated rhythms of Arlen's music.

I have a photograph of Harold and Ted with Eva Kern, Jerry's widow, breaking ground on a new Braille Institute, which would include a Jerome Kern Memorial Music Hall. Arlen and Koehler committed all their royalties from a new song to the project. Once in temple I asked Harold about Ted. He was quiet and methodical, Arlen said. Also practical. Liked helping with the sets and the lights. They called him "Willie Westinghouse." Arlen spoke so warmly of Koehler that I asked him, though I promised my father I wouldn't, why they stopped writing songs together. They had clicked so well. Why break up the partnership? Harold sighed. He had been approached by Yip Harburg and Ira Gershwin, who wanted him to write the music for the revue they eventually called *Life Begins at Eight-Forty*. It was Harold's first crack at writing a Broadway musical. The hard part was telling Ted. He wrote him a letter finally and gave it to him at a Cotton Club rehearsal. What did he say? He reacted just as Harold knew he would. "You'd be a fool if you didn't do it," he said. Did that make him feel better about the end of the partnership? "Not much," said Harold.[23]

IV

Last Night When
We Were Young

Ages ago.

YIP HARBURG, "Last Night When We Were Young"

Uneasy in His Easy Chair

I had the craziest dream and woke to find myself in a tiny downtown apartment. It made me think of the *New Yorker* cartoon with two convicts in a jail cell. Says one to the other, "For a space this size it cost me two thousand a month in Manhattan."

There was Ira Gershwin, courtly as always in his vast overstuffed armchair, though he was already dead, and we sat in the living room and had a friendly conversation. If you think March 31, 1943, was big because of *Oklahoma!* you should have been there on February 12, 1924, in Aeolian Hall in New York, at three in the afternoon, when George played *Rhapsody in Blue* for the first time. What a moment. You know George wanted to write not only popular songs but orchestral works and opera, and he aimed to study with Ravel. But when Ravel found out how much money George made in a year he said, "Maybe I should take lessons from you." You've heard that one? Well, sure.

Ira told me about how many times the family had moved—maybe twenty-five—when he, George, another brother, and a sister were growing up on the Lower East Side. Every family had to have piano or violin lessons for at least one of the children. On Second Avenue, when the upright piano was lifted through the window, George immediately sat down and started to play. He had learned to play on the sly. It was actually bought for me, Ira said, but it took George next to no time to show that he might prove the brighter pupil.[1]

George's sudden death from a misdiagnosed brain tumor hit Ira hard. He had lost an inseparable partner, a brother, a man of undoubted genius. But, then, it hit everyone hard. Even those who didn't especially like George were shocked when the thirty-eight-year-old composer died a few hours after a five-hour emergency operation. "George died on July 1, 1937, but I don't have to believe it if I don't want to," the novelist John O'Hara wrote. Amazingly, some of Ira's best lyrics—"I Can't Get Started" with Vernon Duke, for example—were yet to come.

While we were talking, you could hear George playing in the next room. George was always playing. It wouldn't be a Hollywood party without George at the piano. The piano was his by right of merit. "Tell me, George," his friend Oscar Levant once mocked him, "if you had to do it all over, would you fall in love with yourself again?"[2] But the self-love and the conceit were unobjectionable. He was George, and he was the genuine article. He smoked the big, long, expensive cigars of enjoyment. Lots of girlfriends. But he didn't marry anyone. Why not? Well, Paulette Goddard was already married. And he was very serious about wanting to marry a Jewish woman.[3] I suppose the woman closest to him was Kay Swift. Kay was herself a pianist and composer, very lovely and smart. She wrote "Can't We Be Friends?" Great song. George was nuts about her. It lasted ten years or so, their romance. She said he was the best lover she ever had. And she would have married him. But he wasn't ready to marry her or anyone else. You know what Oscar Levant said when George and Kay entered the room? He said, "Here comes George Gershwin with the future Miss Kay Swift."[4] George liked being a man about town. When one of his romances came to a pretty pass, he chose the way out. The lady would say, Don't you feel bad about the breakup? And he would earnestly explain that he, too, would feel terrible about it, but he was too busy at the moment. Busy with projects, ambitions, hobbies, and a taste for nightlife. He liked going out with Fred Astaire. He and Fred went dancing. And by the way, don't underestimate Astaire's role in our work, Ira said. And not only for us but for Berlin and Mercer and Arlen—all those guys. Ask Irving. Or ask Astaire's buddy, the choreographer Hermes Pan. Berlin told him, "I'd rather have Fred Astaire introduce one of my songs than any other singer I know—not because he has a great voice, but because his delivery and diction are so good that he can put over a song like nobody else."[5] He was the consummate jazz singer, Mel Tormé always said.

As I did with everybody, I asked Ira about Sinatra. Ira recalled the time Sinatra phoned him to see if he would change "The Man That Got Away," written for Judy Garland in *A Star Is Born*, to "The Gal That Got Away" so he could sing it. Usually such opposite-sex versions of songs don't work, Ira said, but this was an exception. Sinatra pointed out that all you needed to do was change "man" to "gal," "his" to "her," and fix the ending. True enough, so I obligingly improvised an ending for him: instead of "a one-man woman" I wrote "a lost, lost loser looking for / The gal that got away." Sinatra liked the alliteration. I thought his recording was excellent, Ira concluded. But such a case of "sex transilience" is rare.

Later, I thought about Ira's point and connected it with something I'd heard from the poet Carolyn Kizer, who was a teenager at the height of the Sinatra craze in the early 1940s. According to Carolyn, what the girls saw in Sinatra was his vulnerability. He had an androgynous side. If he hadn't been so thin, would the girls have loved him so much? Not on your life. He brought out the mother in them. I don't say that in singing to them, he was singing to his mother, or to his mother in them, but androgynous he was, Carolyn said. I thought about this when Ira brought up the "sex transilience" that allowed Sinatra to sing a Judy Garland song. Sinatra was always doing that. "The Girl Next Door." "I Got It Bad and That Ain't Good." A lot of guys might have shied away from singing a girl's song, like "I Could Have Danced All Night" from *My Fair Lady*. Sinatra made it a featured piece of his 1960s concert repertoire.

And by the way, said Ira, the title of that song is "The

Man That Got Away"—"that," not "who." And it's "I Got Rhythm," not "I've got rhythm." Got that? Yes, I did, and I cite it as evidence of Ira's astonishing attention to minute detail, just as the absent comma in the first line of stanza four of "Stopping by Woods on a Snowy Evening" gives evidence of Frost's expertise. (In "The woods are lovely, dark and deep," there should be no serial comma after dark, as if "dark and deep" were twin halves of one adverbial phrase modifying "lovely.") You see, Ira said, the lyricist's task is different from a poet's, and may be more difficult. It's the task of "fitting words mosaically to music already composed." I nodded my head. Having to do that with a Gershwin tune like "My One and Only" or "Fascinating Rhythm" might be the most challenging task of all, I said. And "mosaically" is such a great pun given the influence of your Jewish background. I thanked him for the word. "Don't mention it," he said, which I took to mean "you're welcome," though later when I thought about it I wondered whether he meant that phrase literally. I decided to phone him. After all, there would come a time when I would no longer be able to phone him.

I told Ira that I was dating a dancer and that she had chosen to put on the tape of her telephone answering machine Ella singing the Gershwins' "I'm dancing and I can't be bothered now." Ira looked puzzled. "What's a telephone answering machine?" So I tried a different approach. I said I had called Richard Wilbur on March 1 to wish him a happy eighty-seventh birthday, and when I asked him to name his favorite songs, he told me that "Love Is Here to Stay" is one of the greatest lyrics ever written. I can't believe that Dick

Wilbur is eighty-seven, Ira said gloomily. He told me to pretend, when we went in to see George, that I didn't know that George was dead. It was a secret, Ira said.

Before bidding me good-bye, Ira asked me if I liked riddles. Sure, I said. "Okay," he said. "I have one for you. What do 'They Can't Take That Away from Me,' 'Long Ago and Far Away,' and 'The Man That Got Away' have in common?" Ira Gershwin wrote the lyrics for all three—the first with his brother, the second with Jerome Kern, the third with Harold Arlen. Not one of them won the Academy Award, though all were eligible. "That'll teach me not to write songs with 'away' in their titles," Ira said. "Away with 'away.' "[6]

A Brief Digression on Frank Loesser

My father left his Liberty Street office early one Wednesday afternoon—unheard-of liberty!—and took me to a matinee performance of *How to Succeed in Business Without Really Trying*. We had perfect seats: center orchestra, five rows back. A likable blond actor named Ronnie Welsh had succeeded Robert Morse in the role of Finch, the ambitious book-reading window-washer who charms and connives his way into the highest executive echelons. Michelle Lee played Rosemary, the pretty secretary with the crush on the junior exec on the make. I loved it: the music, the comedy, the satire of business, the exposure of what really goes on in corporate offices. My reaction to the show back then was a little like my reaction these days to *Mad Men*, the cable TV series set in an advertising agency in the early 1960s. I feel a curious nostalgia for the objects of satire. I know we're supposed to disapprove of the smoking, the drinking, the flirting, the benighted attitudes, and yet—all I can say is that after I saw *How to Succeed* I still thought that a business career held what I wanted in life. Of course the music had a lot to do with that. And this makes me realize that I have not spoken nearly enough about the fellow who wrote both the words and the tunes for *How to Succeed*.

Like Cole Porter, Irving Berlin, and a very few others, Frank Loesser was his own lyricist, and a brilliant one at that. Though he cannot match the former in wit or the latter in versatility, Loesser had the musical theater in his blood, and he did write two all-time great Broadway shows: *How to Succeed* (1961) and the peerless *Guys and Dolls* (1950). The volatile, chain-smoking Loesser talked tough and lived hard. Going into showbiz required nothing less than a family rebellion. His parents were very old-school. Secular German Jews from a banking family, they felt that classical music alone was legitimate. Popular song was vulgar and to be avoided by musicians who should know better. Frank's father, Henry, had come to the United States in the 1880s and set himself up as a piano instructor. He is said to have accompanied Lilli Lehmann, the Wagnerian soprano. As a boy Frank learned to sight-sing. He could play by ear and soaked up the music of Bach and Haydn that was a constant presence at home. Mischievous by nature and far from a model student, Loesser got himself expelled from Townsend Harris High School, Ira Gershwin's alma mater, and never took formal music training. Not until many years later did he learn to write music. The family lived in an apartment on West 107th Street.

Frank's half brother Arthur, a concert pianist of considerable renown who was sixteen years older than Frank, would write a gem of a book, *Men, Women and Pianos*, a quirky work of social history so freewheeling in its prose structure and style as to accommodate any number of subjects. Nowhere does he mention Frank, but then again, from Arthur's point of view, the golden age was not when the Gershwins wrote "The Man I Love" or "Lady Be Good," but much further back when all families who could afford to own a piano had a Steinway or a Baldwin in the parlor. The ascent of the radio and the phonograph marked the fall of Arthur's idol, and when the piano was dethroned, it followed that the taste of the public became hopelessly corrupted.[7] Arthur's musical values resembled his parents'; Frank's didn't. One of Frank's daughters said that Frank was everything his mother detested: He was flamboyant, streetwise, loud, and New York Jewish. He smoked Camels like a Russian émigré, drank coffee, and paced. That was his working method. He had a mean temper. Once, when a rehearsal went badly, he walked up to Isabel Bigley, the actress playing Sister Sarah in *Guys and Dolls*, and slapped her across the face.[8]

The New York native began as a lyricist exclusively. Frank was sixteen when his father died, and he quickly took on assorted jobs, writing lyrics among them. Born in 1910, he came of age at a great time for a lover of musicals: He was seventeen and eager in 1927, the year *Hit the Deck*, *A Connecticut Yankee*, *Funny Face*, and *Show Boat* opened on Broadway.[9]

Two years later Loesser published his first lyrics. He went on to work with such talented composers as Hoagy Carmichael ("Two Sleepy People," "Heart and Soul"), Jimmy McHugh ("Let's Get Lost"), and Louis Alter ("Dolores"). One of the first of Frank Sinatra's noteworthy performances with the Tommy Dorsey band, "Dolores" is sweet without being sappy thanks to Loesser's clever use of internal rhyme. When on her balcony Dolores "throws a rose," her loveliness eclipses the "rose she throws." The Dorsey/Sinatra version of "Dolores" rose to number one in 1941, with a competing version by Bing Crosby in second place. A year later came "Let's Get Lost," the happy-go-lucky love song that trumpeter and singer Chet Baker would cover so well that it ended up becoming the title track of a documentary about him. It has the characteristic Loesser insouciance that is so appealing: "Let's defrost in a romantic mist, / Let's get crossed off ev'rybody's list."

Increasingly as World War II ended, Loesser wrote the music as well as the words. He wrote the charming boy-girl duet "Baby, It's Cold Outside," which he and his wife would perform at parties. In 1948 he had his first major Broadway success with *Where's Charley?* a musical adaptation of the play *Charley's Aunt*. Ray Bolger led the audience in "Once in Love with Amy," and the song carried the show for months. In 1950 Loesser became a Broadway immortal with his musical about gamblers and molls out of Damon Runyon's New York, the plot hinging on a sucker bet daring a high roller to take a Salvation Army "doll" to Havana, capital of sin, for a one-night stand. Some musicians favor Loesser's next score, *The Most Happy Fella* (1956), as his most operatic. For *How to Succeed* in

1961, he won a second Tony and, more improbably, a Pulitzer; at the time it was only the fourth musical to be so honored.

Loesser's best lyrics approach the ideal described by Ira Gershwin: "rhymed conversation." Take the elevator scene in *How to Succeed*, where tongue-tied boy and girl tell us what's on their minds as they wait at an elevator bank, their thoughts mediated by the girl's older and wiser friend, who goes back and forth between them saying "Now she's thinking," "And he's thinking." And in short, she wishes he would flirt, and he wonders whether to ask her out, and the one thing they can risk saying aloud is, "Well, it's been a long day." There's a delicious moment in "Happy to Keep His Dinner Warm," sung by Rosemary, who dreams of marrying the boss and moving to the rich New York suburb of New Rochelle. The dream has a great big wink in it. She imagines herself "wearing the wifely uniform," basking in the glow of her young tycoon's "perfectly understandable" neglect. She will wait patiently for the right moment to say "Good evening, dear, / I'm pregnant; what's new with you from downtown?" The semicolon in the last line doesn't begin to do justice to the pregnant pause preceding it.

Loesser wrote for clusters of voices and varied his musical offerings. In *Guys and Dolls* alone there is a fugue for horse-racing touts, a male and female apology-and-complaint duet, a female-solidarity duet, a striptease, a supplication to the muse of fortune, a takeoff on a rousing gospel song, and an ode to the city as it looks "a couple of deals before dawn"— in addition to the up-tempo male duet that is the title track and the love songs for two voices. The genius of *Guys and*

Dolls is that it captures the vitality of New York City and presents the audience with an uncanny image of itself: The men are commitment-averse gamblers, and the women fall into two categories. On one side is Sister Sarah, the Salvation Army major in uniform, a figure of rectitude, charity, and good sense. On the other side is Miss Adelaide, the burlesque queen who gets to sing one of Broadway's most durable showstoppers, "Adelaide's Lament." When, toward the end of the show, the two women get together to sing "Marry the Man Today"—a song that was left out of the movie—it represents the allegorical union of these two opposing types. The united female psyche! They are sisters after all and, like all heroines of musical comedy, worshipers of the god of marriage. In the course of that satiric song, Loesser has the girls name the "respectable" components of the proper bourgeois life: "*Reader's Digest!* Guy Lombardo! Rogers Peet! Golf! Galoshes! Ovaltine!"[10] There you have the 1950s in ten words or less. Greater composers than Loesser never wrote a sustained musical comedy half as good or as enduring as *Guys and Dolls*. I am not alone in maintaining that *Guys and Dolls* is the ultimate Broadway musical comedy, just as *South Pacific* is either the ultimate Broadway operetta or a close second. Nor is it an accident that they opened less than two years apart, *South Pacific* at the Majestic Theatre on April 7, 1949, and *Guys and Dolls* at the 46th Street Theatre on November 24, 1950.[11]

Nothing Rhymes with Kennedy

My piano pals and I used to have heated discussions over the standing of these songwriters. Would Richard Rodgers surpass his idol, Jerome Kern? Does Arlen measure up to George Gershwin? Was Alec Wilder right to say that Ira's lyric for " 'S Wonderful" was better than George's music? What do you think of Sammy Cahn?

Some wag called Sammy the "eleventh best lyricist in Hollywood," a left-handed compliment that said a lot about the ferocity of the competition. Cahn was born Samuel Cohen in 1913 to refugees who came from Galicia "around 1905, 1907," according to Sammy, who is nothing if not frank about the social status of his tribe. "To be a Galitzianer was to be the lowest kind of Jew."[12] I once heard that his ex-wife said Sammy was just like Sinatra "except without the looks and without the voice," a pretty tough crack to make about Frank's go-to guy when a lyric was needed instantly. Some say Sammy talked too much and too many sentences began with "I," but I ate it up. Sammy was haimish, a gabber, who always had time for you and never failed to remind you that when the great Johnny Mercer grew too ill to discharge his duties as president of the songwriters' association, Mercer himself tapped Cahn for the position.

Ask Sammy which came first, the words or the music, and he'll either say "the money" or "the phone call," or if he is in a rare decorous mood and you represent a major newsmagazine he'll say "the request." Cahn wrote with great facility. He could bang out parody lyrics as fast as Sinatra needed them for, say, a duet with Van Johnson on the radio or a toast to Edward G. Robinson on his birthday. The Van Johnson duet was just after the war, and the tune Cahn lampooned was "Personality" (music Jimmy Van Heusen, words Johnny Burke).

> Sinatra: "It's not my place to make this crack. / But I hear tell that Gable's back."
> Johnson: "Frankie, here's a bromo."
> Sinatra: "Why?"
> Johnson: "A Como."

Cahn teamed up with Jule Styne early on and with Van Heusen later, and the first priority of both partnerships was to meet the vocal needs of Frank Sinatra. Cahn wrote the words for "Saturday Night Is the Loneliest Night in the Week," "Five Minutes More," "Come Out Wherever You Are," and "Time After Time" (with Styne) and for "Love and Marriage," "The Second Time Around," "(Love Is) The Tender Trap," and "My Kind of Town" (with Van Heusen). He had the knack of telling a story in thirty-two bars, as in "The Things We Did Last Summer" and "Guess I'll Hang My Tears Out to Dry." There's a touching part in the latter where the anguished lover's friends advise him to forget her, the girl who broke his heart, and the strategy worked well enough until "one day she passed him right by." The words are simple, the sentence ordinary, but there's a narrative kick to the lyric. The song is a cousin of Hoagy Carmichael's "I Get Along Without You Very Well." No wonder Sinatra liked singing them both. Pure heartbreak in the saloon of life.

When I encountered Sammy he was still sore at Sinatra for missing his son's bar mitzvah. He sounded very solemn about it. It was funny. But then Sammy was naturally humorous, a man of "loud and lasting yocks" and ceaseless patter. The apartment he and Phil Silvers shared in the Piccadilly Hotel on West 45th Street when they were young and carefree was so small "you had to step outside to change your mind." (I think he may have gotten that one from Henny Youngman.)[13] Sammy has a riff on the "smart Jew syndrome"—the assumption that all Jews are smart. "I have proof positive that the Jews are *not* the smartest people in the world," he says. "My father wasn't smart." I asked Sammy about the time he persuaded Sinatra to do one more take of "(Love Is) The Tender Trap"—the terrific one you can hear today on *The Capitol Years.* How did he get him to do it? I asked, thinking of Sinatra's reputation for intransigence and a quick temper. "Frank said he couldn't reach the high F on 'love' at the end of the song. I said, 'Sure you can.' He gave me the famous Sinatra glare. I said, 'You *have* to do it. *You're Frank Sinatra.*' "

Once Sammy started talking there was no stopping him. I spent afternoons with Sinatra, he said, but I never went with him, you know what I mean? If you went with him you had to be ready at a moment's notice for the phone call. Frank is taking off for Las Vegas in eighteen minutes, or Frank is going to Jilly's, or whatever. Then the phone rang. Sammy sounded very firm. "I know you want me to have a word with him," he said, "but I can't work miracles. He retired, and when he makes up his mind, that's it." Sammy said, "Where was I? Sinatra. He was always after me to write parody lyrics for his New Year's Eve party or whatever, and I always came through." I told Sammy that I remember seeing the Kennedy campaign entourage, including Jackie, singing the theme song of the 1960 presidential campaign to the tune of "High Hopes." "You know how I wrote that? Nothing rhymes with Kennedy, so I spelled out his name, 'K E double-N E D Y, Jack's the nation's favorite guy.' That was one of my four Oscars: 'High Hopes.' One I had with Jule, the other three with Jimmy, and Sinatra sang them all. 'Call Me Irresponsible' was the last one. Full of five-syllable words—irresponsible, unreliable, undependable, undeniably—and I'm from a one-syllable neighborhood. Do you know what Cole Porter said to me? He said he could have been a genius if he had been born like me on the Lower East Side. Imagine: a world-class WASP from Indiana, not to mention a brilliant alumnus of Yale University, a true genius, envying me, a *pisher* from the Lower East Side!

"You know how I write a lyric? The melody flashes a title into my head and the title triggers the lyric. And almost always the music comes first, though there are exceptions—'Tender Trap' was one."[4] The phone rang. Sammy said, "Not tonight," and hung up.

I asked Sammy about the verse of a song and why singers sometimes skip it, even when it's excellent. "The verse," he said, "is just the preface to the chorus, that's all it is. For every verse there ever was you can substitute one phrase: 'and that's why I say. . . .' Think about it. And that's why I say . . . Come fly with me! And that's why I say . . . I'll walk alone."[5]

"I see," I said. "Answer me another. How come all the great Christmas songs, like 'Let It Snow, Let It Snow, Let It Snow,' were written on hot summer days?"

"We had to do it that way," Sammy said. "Timing. If you were going to make a record for Christmas sales, you had to get started by the Fourth of July to give everyone time to learn the music, rehearse, get it together. Tell me the truth. Do you like that song?"

"Yes," I said. "I heard Sinatra do it slow with a muted piano accompaniment, and it was like an intimate love song." Sammy beamed. "And," I continued, "my favorite moment in the Bruce Willis *Die Hard* movies is when Vaughn Monroe sings 'Let It Snow, Let It Snow, Let It Snow' over the closing credits. It's been a running gag throughout the films."

"I didn't know that," Sammy said.

"Well"—I shrugged my shoulders apologetically—"it happened a few years before you died." Then I told him my theory that Harold Arlen's pop could adapt Jule Styne's melody for 'Let It Snow, Let It Snow, Let It Snow' to the Hebrew liturgy for the closing of the ark after the reading of the Torah. Sammy laughed. When you're an only son, a lot is expected of you in a Jewish family. "If there are four sons and one gets convicted for murder and goes to the electric chair, well, you still have three shots at one becoming a doctor or a lawyer," Sammy explained. "But you're an only son and you become a songwriter, the odds are against you." The phone rang. He picked it up irritably. "Just a minute. This one I've got to take, boychik." I thought for a moment he was going to pinch my cheek. "You know who you should talk to?" he said.

"Who?" I said.

"My old partner, Jule Styne," and he closed the door.[16]

This was a great tip because I loved Styne's music, the stuff written with Cahn for Sinatra and the theater scores of Broadway shows he did in the 1950s: *Gentlemen Prefer Blondes* (lyrics Leo Robin), *Bells Are Ringing* (Betty Comden and Adolph Green), and *Gypsy* (Stephen Sondheim). The cliché about Styne's music is that it's brassy, so let's avoid that and just say that after Helen Forrest sings the chorus of a Jule Styne number, a Harry James trumpet solo may follow. According to Max Wilk in *They're Playing Our Song*, one of Styne's collaborators likened working with Jule to "driving in a small sports car, with the windows closed and the top up, and you're in the mountains, and you go down a pass at seventy miles an hour, your brakes are locked, you're skidding—and all the time there's this hornet inside the car with you, buzzing around your head. That buzzing is Jule!"

Like Cahn, Styne—born Julius Kerwin Stein in London in 1905—was a world-class chatterbox. His parents, who had emigrated from the Ukraine, owned a grocery store. When he was six, they arranged for him to take piano lessons with a teacher from the London Conservatory of Music. Two years later, the family came to America, to Chicago, and young Jule quickly made a name for himself as a piano prodigy. The drama of his adolescence was his rejection of classical music in favor of playing with bands. But he always maintained that the decision was made for him when he damaged the second finger of his right hand in a factory accident. At the age of twenty-one, he wrote his first song, "Sunday," to impress a girl. The song sold half a million copies of sheet music. It's excellent: Listen to Sinatra's version on *Swing Easy.* Jule liked smoking cigarettes almost as much as his buddy Frank Loesser. I asked him what made him work so well with Cahn and he talked about Sammy's instinct. He can hear a tune and immediately a phrase seems to jump into his head, and he builds his lyric around that. For example, the first time they met, Styne played him a song he had started to write with Loesser. Cahn hears a few bars and shouts "I heard that song." I said never, no one ever heard it. No, he said. "We're going to call it 'I've Heard That Song Before.' " They did, and it went to the top of the charts.[17]

Of Styne's theater songs my favorite is probably "Diamonds Are a Girl's Best Friend" as Carol Channing did it. Leo Robin, not the most prolific of lyricists but one of the best, wrote the words. Robin paced as he talked. "The music guys could write a lot faster than the word guys," he said. "They could write fast. Rodgers could write a number—and not just any but the big exotic one that would help make a show—between dessert and port. I'm talking about 'Bali Ha'i.' Well, some of the lyricists could give them a run for the money. Larry Hart wrote fast if Dick could get him to sit still long enough. You met Irving Caesar, who wrote the lyrics for Gershwin's first hit. He and George knocked off 'Swanee' in about eleven minutes. At least that's what Irving says. Did he tell you how he wrote 'Tea for Two' in his sleep? Vincent Youmans came knocking in the middle of the night with this new tune for *No, No, Nanette*. Everyone felt the show was pretty good but lacked the one showstopper that could turn it into a hit. Caesar, grouchy, wrote a dummy lyric on the spot, and it turned out to be the immortal 'tea for two / and two for tea' of everlasting glory. Did you know that Isham Jones got a new piano as a present from his wife, and to celebrate he wrote four songs that night? Two of them were 'It Had to Be You' and 'The One I Love Belongs to Somebody Else.' Gus Kahn wrote the lyrics for both, but I can tell you this. Gus wrote fast, but he didn't polish off those babies in a night. Be sure you write about Gus. Mercer called 'It Had to Be You' the ideal lyric. He could be right. You know—'With all your faults, I love you still.' Gus was Walter Donaldson's ideal lyricist. Have you seen *Love Me or Leave Me*? That's what they called the movie of Ruth Etting's life with Doris Day playing Ruth Etting and singing those great old songs. It's very good. Incidentally, the stereotype of Doris is all wrong. Oscar Levant joked, 'I knew Doris Day before she was a virgin.' This movie is from the before time. She's a true songbird. Me? I'm a little unconventional. People say 'Thanks for the Memory' was my best. Bob Hope thought so. You know who loves my lyrics? Susannah McCorkle. Have you heard her? She proves cabaret lives." I replied that I had bought her CD devoted to his lyrics. But I didn't want to tell him about her shocking death. She flung herself out the window of her Upper West Side apartment. Well, he said. Leaving time is grieving time. I don't like good-byes any more than your uncle Harold does.

Blues in the Night

Harold Arlen died inconsolable in 1986. There was plenty of reason for him to feel dejected. All you had to do was turn on the radio. They weren't playing Gershwin, Rodgers, Kern, Berlin, or Porter. No more "Sentimental Journey" with Les Brown and his band of renown except on "music of your life" AM channels in the sticks. What were they playing instead? Noise. Arlen called it *farkakteh*, an untranslatable term somewhere between "nonsense" and "bullshit," and that was back in the early 1970s. Irving Berlin said he felt like putting up a sign saying he had closed down shop. Imagine the crises various individuals went through. No work, no demand, and for singers there was the inevitable conflict of whether to try singing the new rock songs. Very sad to hear Sinatra at a concert saying something wildly insincere and hyperbolic about a bland George Harrison song ("Something"); even worse, try listening to the old man's recording of Petula Clark's "Downtown." Mel Tormé joked that he was in a state of mel torment. For a while in the late 1960s Mel, who had an aircraft license, entertained the notion of giving up singing in favor of becoming an airline pilot. I'm not kidding. Tony Bennett tried to adapt to the new material, but his 1969 album *Tony Sings the Great Hits of Today!* pleased no one, and with his personal life in disarray, he developed a drug habit that nearly killed him before he turned his life around in 1979. The fiddlers had fled, leaving a hefty bill.

"In just about the span of twenty-five years the whole lovely, warm-hearted, clear-headed, witty, bittersweet world of the professional songwriter was gone," Alec Wilder wrote in his chapter on Arlen in *American Popular Song*.[18] Wilder blamed the "amateurs," the kids with guitars. That was back in 1972. Here's Will Friedwald's take on how pop music has fared since the early 1950s: "Our standard of living rose, and our standard of culture generally plummeted. This was nowhere truer than in pop music, not only in the debasements of the blues that were being packaged for kiddie consumption, but also in the older styles of American pop that were being beaten to death by over-powerful, hit-happy producers."[19]

There were and are pockets of resistance, attempts to fuse the musical styles of the 1940s with recent postmodernist narrative techniques. Dennis Potter's six-hour television series, *The Singing Detective* (1986), is a fusion of memory, dream, fantasy, hard-boiled detective story, and lip-synching wizardry. The characters open their mouths and out come the voices of the Ink Spots singing "Into Each Life Some Rain Must Fall" or Dick Haymes singing "It Might as Well Be Spring," songs that were popular in 1945, the year the action takes place. A periodic revival of interest in Sinatra or Tony Bennett, an homage to Nat King Cole by Diana Krall, new recordings of jazz standards by the likes of Steve Tyrell or Rebecca Kilgore, classes in swing dancing, the sound track of a Woody Allen movie, the work of dedicated disc jockeys with a taste for Jack Jones or Vic Damone all extend the life of the music. But we have crossed the line from having a living art form to one that endures in repertory. When

Broadway aficionado Ethan Mordden calls *Hair* a "disaster without end" and says that the golden age of the Broadway musical is over, his *New York Times* interviewer asks him whether he is immune from the tendency to overpraise the past and resist what is new. Many of us ask ourselves the same question. Mordden's answer is persuasive: "I don't believe that older people in the 1920s, when Kern and Berlin were joined by the Gershwins and all those great people, would say 'Whatever happened to Karl Hoschna?' or 'Why can't they write a score like *The Prince of Pilsen*? I think they were saying, 'God, this new stuff is good.' "[20] For many, the change in popular music has been calamitous. Jo Stafford offered this analysis in 1982:

> When the Presleys and other first, popular, legend-in-their-own-time performers started to come along it was the first time in the U.S. where a ten-year-old had enough money to influence something to the extent that they did. So when you've got a ten-year-old picking the music, it's going to be pretty simple. Just above the level of a nursery rhyme. The other music is too sophisticated for young ears. I'm not being judgmental at all; it's a simple statement of fact that that's the first time kids had enough money to influence a market and they did.[21]

"In the age of Elvis, popular music dispensed with interesting and beautiful harmony," Gene Lees argues in his biography of Johnny Mercer, *Portrait of Johnny*. "In the age of rap, it dispensed even with melody, beautiful or otherwise, developing a form of badly rhymed chant advocating mayhem, mutilation, and murder. It's truly ugly stuff. And radio evolved in such a way that it is impossible to find anything by Kern on the air, and jazz has disappeared from commercial radio broadcasting." The gloomy assessment continues for another paragraph.[22]

But who wants to sound like a grumpy old man, nostalgic for a golden age there never was? Not I. How well I recall the response to Wilfrid Sheed's book on the fate of the American songbook, *The House That George Built*. The critics loved it, mainly; it was full of wry or sharp observations, and laced with passionate, sometimes ornery opinions. Yet even an admiring reviewer has to get in a lick, and Sheed was taxed more than once for not evincing enough sympathy for the musical styles that have recently come to the fore. Toward the end of his laudatory and perceptive review of Sheed's book, Robert Gottlieb writes, "How regrettable, it seems to me, that a man with such generous, perceptive love for George's and Irving's and Cole's house should miss out on the pleasures of Motown, for instance, or from Hank Williams, or Bob Dylan, or Carole King and Gerry Goffin, or for all I know, from rap."[23] To lament the decline of the jazz standard is to risk sounding academically or culturally incorrect in the same way that a liking for Somerset Maugham's novels (especially when combined with an instinctive dislike of French literary theory) marks one as incorrect or, worse, retrograde—one who clings to the view that melody in a song, like narrative in a story, is a powerful tool that the composer should not discard lightly. Better to remind oneself of the peril of idealizing the past by focusing on its accomplishments and conveniently overlooking its drawbacks. There will be days when you feel like lamenting the passing of so many of the things that made the experience of being a grown-up in 1948 superior to what we have in its place today. Nevertheless I guarantee you that a day of the popular culture in 1948 was as dumb as a day defined by the media in 2008 and that an American Jew ran greater risks in the 1940s than in any decade since.

The more respectable view is that the decline of "superior classic pop songs" is overdetermined and not simply a sign that the sensibility of the public has grown more juvenile. It was also that the baby-boom generation wanted something different from pop music. A revenge song from the 1930s could make you chuckle. In "Goody, Goody," which Helen Ward sang for the Benny Goodman orchestra in 1936, the Johnny Mercer lyric rhymes "hooray and hallelujah" with "you had it comin' to ya." In 1967, when Country Joe and the Fish rhymed "Vietnam" and "don't give a damn," it was funny in an altogether different way—it was a species of gallows humor, full of sound and fury. A less distinguished but equally angry rock-and-roll song announced the eve of destruction and equated the "hate" in Red China with that in Selma, Alabama. Nothing funny about that. Rock and roll had body to it (the hips of Elvis), and it had enormous ambition; it wanted to make a statement, and it didn't mind seeming naïve. "Where Have All the Flowers Gone?" and "Blowin' in the Wind" were not about the problems of two people worth a hill of beans in this crazy world of ours but about the folly of war and the demand for social justice for all. The new music devalued cleverness and irony, not to mention the clarinet and the trombone. In their stead it

offered an incessant sexual beat, an eardrum-splitting deci-
bel level, and the fury of protest. Alcohol had entered the
American standards in saloon songs like "Angel Eyes" or in
jolly party tunes like Cole Porter's "Well, Did You Evah?"
Drugs performed a similar function in rock and roll. Songs
like "White Rabbit" (Jefferson Airplane), "Strange Brew"
(Cream), and "Lucy in the Sky with Diamonds" (the Beatles) could get you high with or without the kiss of Mary Jane
to deepen the experience. To cap it off, the Beatles and Bob
Dylan erased the distinction between writer and performer,
and made it seem artificial and superfluous. This was considered a major advance: *They wrote their own material!* One academic analysis has it that a jazz standard, "Night and Day"
or "Body and Soul," is like a Keats sonnet while the singer-
songwriters who wrote their own material were more like
Byronic authors of personal epics. It's an inspired analogy,
though not an altogether convincing one.[24]

Yet, though I warm to Motown and Carole King as well as
Dylan among the recent musical "pleasures" Gottlieb lists in
his review of Sheed, I know, too, that an ode to the great
songwriters is bound to turn elegiac. Nor can this be merely
an instance of the universal longing for the world as it
existed before our presence on the scene. Whether the chief
cause was television or teenage rebellion or something else
entirely, the fact was that when the old songwriters went out
of business, a whole culture came to an end. Nightclubs
closed, ballroom dancing went out of style, and the Broadway show as a genre almost went belly up (except as a
tourist attraction). Swing jazz, big band music, the lindy
and the fox-trot, and the art of the vocalist endure but as

specialty or "niche" preferences, marginal to the culture as a whole. There was a moment when you could turn on the radio at random and routinely hear Anita O'Day sing "Love Me or Leave Me" or Margaret Whiting sing "Hit the Road to Dreamland." That moment is gone.

I decided I had better talk to these people, to Sammy Cahn and Jule Styne and the rest while there was still time. That's when I started this project. I took notes, made tapes, listened to records, read books. But I also had a life to live and a living to make, and the project gathered dust. Now, years later, I mean to make good on that early promise. I will write up my love of American popular song and its Jewish creators and I will write it straight, leaving myself out of it. It will be an elegy, but it will also burst with facts and anecdotes, observations and arguments, and maybe it will help a little in the struggle to keep the music going. That's key. After all, the songs rank with Hollywood studio movies as the signal American cultural achievement of the last century, ahead of Abstract Expressionism, jazz, and modern poetry if only because the work of art with a wide and vital audience may be deemed superior to the work of art for the "fit audience but few." Milton is great, but Shakespeare is even greater.

I Hear Music

There are days when the songs blend into one another in my mind as I cross the streets of downtown Manhattan. It's as if I alone can hear the medley, an effect I would like to reproduce as best I can with a cento—a poem consisting of lines lifted from other poems, in this case the titles of songs. Some of the titles are joined together by the rhetorical maneuver known as the zeugma, in which one word links two disparate things—the way "or" works in Alexander Pope's line "Or stain her honor or her new brocade."

"Poem in the Manner of a Jazz Standard"

I've got five dollars and my love to keep me warm
I've got the world on a string and you under my skin
You're the cream in my coffee and driving me crazy
    You couldn't be cuter and go to my head

Love is here to stay and just around the corner
Where or when I take my sugar to tea
All I do is dream of you, all of you,
    You took advantage of all of me

Don't blame me or worry 'bout me
It had to be you and might as well be spring
Let's get away from it all, fall in love, face the music
    And dance with me, let's do it

I got rhythm and the right to sing the blues
She didn't say yes she's funny that way
I believe in you were never lovelier
    My melancholy baby my shining hour

V

I Didn't Know What Time It Was

And now I know I was naïve.

LORENZ HART, "I Didn't Know What Time It Was"

The summer I graduated from Stuyvesant High School, the Sinatra song on the radio was "Strangers in the Night," but if you bought the 45 you got the real treat on the flip side: "Summer Wind." That June I went to Camp Terpsichore in East Greenbush, New York, where I was the counselor in charge of putting out the camp newspaper to be distributed to one and all as they boarded the buses on the way home. At Terpsichore my old friend Noah Rosenblatt was the music and dance counselor, who played piano during the shows the campers put on. He also directed them, assisted by me. We staged *The Wizard of Oz* for kids between eight and thirteen and *Guys and Dolls* for the older bunks. In September, we went our separate ways, he to Brandeis and I to Columbia.

At eight every morning that fall I boarded the Number One train on the elevated platform at Dyckman Street with my cuffed khakis and button-down blue oxford shirt and my copy of Shakespeare's *Sonnets* open to number 55. But when I got out of the subway at 116th Street and Broadway, the mood had changed to sonnet number 87, and the sound track changed accordingly. Rock and roll had decisively defeated jazz and transformed the nature of popular song. The singers I loved—Sinatra, Ella, Tormé, Nat Cole, and the rest—were all part of the old regime, to be quietly abandoned if not rejected outright in the way that a lot of things, good and bad and neutral, were ditched: crew cuts and *Lassie*, virginity and men's hats, the cha-cha and the study of foreign languages and other course requirements. The joint displaced the cocktail. Vietnam replaced World War II as the objective correlative of modern war. The Pill had changed the dating and mating habits of a generation, altering people's behavior, tastes, and definition of female beauty, and we went overnight from Ava Gardner and Kim Novak to Mia Farrow and Twiggy. It sounds simpleminded and naïve when I sum it up this way, but at the time a lot of us thought that something resembling a cultural revolution was in the works, that its effects were going to be permanent and for the better, and that its primary agents were rock and roll, marijuana, acid, mescaline, long hair, and sexual promiscuity. Just watch *Easy Rider* (1969), and you'll see. You can't miss the importance of the music ("Born to Be Wild," "Wasn't Born to Follow," "Groovin'," "With a Little Help from My Friends") as a herald of the political and personal liberation pursued by the movie's motorcycle-riding heroes and vicariously by the audience. I was watching it the other day and noticed again how earnest the picture is in embracing its pieties. Consider the moment Peter Fonda compliments an unsmiling farmer: "You're doing your own thing in your own time. You should be proud." Jack Nicholson, then unknown, steals the show. Wearing a college jersey with a giant "M" on it, he is raving about UFOs when he gets stoned on grass for the very first time. That was far out, maybe the best marijuana scene in the movies.

To be a lyricist under the changed circumstances of the time required that you play the guitar, acoustic or electric, with an affinity for either folk music or rock and roll or some blend of the two. None of the instruments I had failed to master (piano, clarinet, trombone, string bass) were in demand. At high school socials and summer camp mixers, the dancers weren't going to hold their partners or listen to the words. It was easier to dance in the new solitary shake-all-over way, so I didn't complain, though I secretly preferred the steps I had learned in dance lessons. But then I didn't know what time it was; I was too busy learning the blues—blue skies, blue moon, blues in the night. Introspective, self-conscious, and shy, I was never really comfortable at parties or bars, too involved in books and the acquisition of knowledge, even more deeply involved in my own mind, and too attached to an obsolete idea of adulthood. "I'm old-fashioned" was a terrible pickup line in 1967. Various girlfriends tried to educate me in the virtues of the Mamas and the Papas and Joni Mitchell, and I did my best to fit in. My coolest literary friends liked the Rolling Stones, who won me over with their arrogant narcissism and aggression. On a July day in 1969 the dead body of the Stones' guitarist Brian Jones turned up at the bottom of his swimming pool. The police said he had drunk a cocktail of drugs and drinks, but whispers of foul play circulated avidly. In Hyde Park I heard Mick Jagger read a stanza of Shelley's "Adonais" before the group kicked off their free concert with "Jumping Jack Flash" and other songs of defiant selves, backstreet girls, and failed connections. If ever a band and its audience were perfectly in tune, it was that summer day in London. The huge crowd heard the news that rape and murder were "just a shot away" and reacted with unforced jubilation.

Exactly four summers earlier at Camp Terpsichore, Noah Rosenblatt had turned me on to Bob Dylan. We listened to *Bringing It All Back Home* and *Highway 61 Revisited* as though to forbidden knowledge. We compared the narrative of Abraham in Dylan's song with that in Genesis, and we caught a whiff of the menace or threat that went together well with the songwriter's put-on sarcasm. In the title track of *Highway 61 Revisited*, Abraham, when called, doesn't say "here I am," and God doesn't command him to "Take now thy son, thine only son, whom thou lovest, even Isaac" and "offer" him upon a mountain in Moriah. Dylan's God bluntly says "kill me a son" and "Abe" replies "man you must be puttin' me on." Abraham the patriarch has become Abe, honest Abe, an everyman, and God, addressed in the vernacular as "man," has become a diminished entity reigning over a diminished universe. Any son will do for the desired offering. Note the sacred individuality of the biblical Isaac: "thy son, thine only son, whom thou lovest." The Isaac of Genesis observes the fire and the wood and wonders about the absence of the lamb for the offering, and his father majestically responds, "God will provide." But Isaac in Dylan's song doesn't exist: he is "a son," any son. The biblical Abraham has faith equal to doubt. But this is Highway 61 revisited: the dawn of a new age (1961) seen in retrospect four years later. The handsome young president has been assassinated, the New Frontier has given way to the Great Society, and LBJ has escalated the war in Vietnam. Facing the threat of coercion, Abe progresses rapidly from incredulity to acquiescence. Where shall he perform the bloody deed? Not on a mountaintop but on Highway 61. Noah and I thought of a place with the same number of syllables as "sixty-one": Vietnam. Anything irreverent and antiauthoritarian we related to that stupid helicopter war and the body bags coming back and LBJ stubborn in the Oval Office and the protestors outside repeating his initials and chanting "How many kids did you kill today?"

With a straight face Dylan toyed with all the Joneses out there who knew something was happening but didn't know what. Dylan perfected a method of speaking that has served him well to this day. "I was gonna talk out both sides of my mouth and what you heard depended on which side you were standing."¹

Dylan shared much with the Jewish songwriters of the earlier generation, and he knew it. In *Chronicles: Volume One*, Dylan recalls his pleasure in hearing Judy Garland ("from Grand Rapids, Minnesota, a town about twenty miles away from where I came from") singing Harold Arlen songs. "In Harold's songs, I could hear rural blues and folk music. There was an emotional kinship there." Woody Guthrie "ruled my universe," but "I could never escape from the bittersweet, lonely intense world of Harold Arlen."² Like Harold, Dylan—whose grandmother came to America from

Odessa—renamed himself, though "Bob Dylan" was not just a name but a persona, an invention. The Dylan of 1965 was totally secular, emblematic of the counterculture, yet he remained Jewish in the moral ire and indignation he could summon and vent. He had something of the old-fashioned Old Testament prophet about him. He wrote and sang about taking drugs and breaking up with a woman and the acceleration of social change and how certain injustices cried out for remedy. But it was his devastating hostility that drew me most. "You got a lotta nerve," he tells a friend who betrayed him, and the rhyme of "got a" and "lotta" speeds you to your destination: rejection of the false one, the envious Iago. That was "Positively Fourth Street." The anger has lost none of its bite in forty years. In "Maggie's Farm," Maggie's brother has always embodied the small-time boss, not as imposing a creature as the "white man boss" of "Ol' Man River" but kin, the sort who hands you small change, smirks when he talks, and fines you whenever you slam the door. What liberation to announce, "I ain't gonna work for Maggie's brother no more."

As we had a day off coming to us, Noah suggested that we drive to Rhode Island and attend the Newport Folk Festival. Two other counselors joined us in a rickety car that needed a new muffler, and Noah was the only one of us with a license. After six hours on the road we got to Newport on the night that Bob Dylan scandalized the audience by playing "Like a Rolling Stone." He had gone electric—heresy to folk music purists—and some people booed. I liked what I heard. The concert ended, and I had absolutely no idea that we had watched and heard something historic, an iconic moment.

I remember little of the evening except how tired I was when we got back in the jalopy and how hard it was to stay awake and keep Noah awake for the six hours it took to drive back to camp in the middle of the night "with no direction home," way past curfew, a "complete unknown." We repeated the words "how does it feel" accusingly. On the radio, we listened to new reports about riots breaking out in the Watts section of Los Angeles. It was 1965. Our absence was noted at camp, and my punishment was that I would not get to be the general of my team in color war that summer, plus Noah and I and the other two were to be "OD" for a week. "On Duty" meant patrolling the campus with a flashlight while the younger campers slept in their cabins and most of the counselors went to the cocktail lounge at the local bowling alley and drank vodka collinses. At the time, going to the cocktail longe was a lot more important to me than the Dylan performance at Newport.

The other music counselor went home early that summer, and I was drafted into playing the piano for the production of *Carousel* that the counselors and waiters were doing. Luckily I knew the score.

Camp Paradox

"I knew the score." For a lyricist it's hard to resist the pun whether you're writing a song for Sky Masterson in *Guys and Dolls* or for a saloon singer whose baby just gave him the air. The phrase can lead you down to the depths of a dirge. But I mean it literally. Memorizing the score of *Carousel* at summer camp got me almost obsessively interested in the works and days of the man who composed it, Richard Rodgers.

After Kern and Arlen, Rodgers was the composer I liked the most. The son of a well-to-do doctor, Rodgers was the author of a long list of jazz standards (though he hated swing), the composer of numerous immortal Broadway musicals, and the producer or co-producer of many others. I've heard it said that somewhere in the world twice a day the curtain goes up on a new production of *Oklahoma!* I have sworn off the phrase "transcend the genre" or else I'd quote somebody saying that the best of Rodgers and Hammerstein transcends musical comedy just as Gilbert and Sullivan transcended the music-hall conventions of late nineteenth-century London. For thirty-five years—from 1925 until Hammerstein's death in 1960—Rodgers set the gold standard on the Hardened Artery (as Walter Winchell dubbed Broadway), and in all that time he worked with only two partners.[3]

Dick Rodgers seldom went to services, and I knew my father disapproved, but he still respected the man for being a gentleman who had done a lot for the Jews just by being one. I idolized him and his partners in rhyme, Hart and Hammerstein. Rodgers collaborated with the first for twenty-four years and with the second for the next seventeen. At fifteen Dick saw the Columbia varsity show and decided right then and there that his life's ambition was to go to Columbia and write the college's varsity show. Here's how it happened. Morty Rodgers, already a Columbia undergrad, brought his younger brother to the Hotel Astor in March 1917 to see *Home, James.* After the show Morty took Dick backstage and introduced him to his friend the law student who had written most of the libretto. The friend's name was Oscar Hammerstein II, and in later years he liked to say with a wide grin that his future collaborator, for whom he would someday write the lyrics for "I'm Just a Girl Who Can't Say No" and "There Is Nothing Like a Dame," was still wearing short pants that evening in 1917. Dick flatly denied this.

Summer camps played a bigger part in these guys' lives than people realize. Dick Rodgers spent his summers with Herbert Fields, brother of Dorothy, at Camp Paradox in the Adirondacks, where they wrote the Sunday shows. Camp Paradox! Can there possibly be a better name for a summer camp? Never mind that it owed its name to its location, Lake Paradox, where camp legend has it that the water flows in the wrong direction. With all the added connotations that "camp" has acquired over the years, Camp Paradox could serve as the title of a Broadway show about a bunch of young Jewish geniuses who wanted to re-create themselves as Americans and wound up re-creating American culture in the process. No rest but plenty of recreation at Camp Paradox, where Rodgers, at age eighteen, wore his Camp Paradox T-shirt and smiled for the camera with his brother Morty at his side. That summer Dick was getting paid to write a musical production and present it every Sunday night.

What kind of place was Camp Paradox? According to a brochure,

a mere narrative of equipment and camp activities gives but a poor picture of Camp life. The element which vitalizes the incidents of a summer in Paradox, is the wholesome and hearty enthusiasm and loyalty which are felt by each and every camper. This reflection of college spirit is the moving cause of Camp songs, Camp cheers, and of meetings and rallies on every occasion. While the spirit is difficult to describe, it is this feeling which arouses the enthusiasm of each camper during the summer, and causes the memory of a season at Paradox, as well as the close friendships formed, to endure throughout the winter.

With Jo Stafford's golden voice singing "The Things We Did Last Summer" (music Jule Styne, lyrics Sammy Cahn) in the background, I ask you: Could Rimbaud have improved on a "summer in Paradox"? It sounds like a quote from T. S. Eliot's essay on the metaphysical poets. In 1917, a season in Paradox, running from the end of June to the beginning of September, would have cost your parents $250.

Earlier, Rodgers spent some summers at Camp Wigwam, where fellow campers included Stephen Sondheim's father and David O. Selznick, producer of *Gone with the Wind* and *Rebecca*, which won back-to-back best-picture Oscars in 1939 and 1940. Frank Loesser's half brother Arthur was one of the music counselors at Wigwam the summer that Rodgers wrote the camp song "Campfire Days." That was the summer of 1916. Dick was fourteen. When he was still younger, he went to Weingart's Institute in Highmount, New York, where he narrowly missed meeting both of his future collaborators. It was, in fact, at Weingart's that Oscar Hammerstein II met Lorenz Hart, who edited the camp newspaper, *Review*. Hart also put in time at Wigwam, and when he spent a summer at Camp Paradox, the other kids called him Shakespeare, because he arrived with a trunk packed with books, including a complete Shakespeare, and no clothes.

Readers with camp-age children may want to know that Camp Paradox remains a going concern, as does Brant Lake Camp in the Adirondacks. In his twenties, Larry Hart would take vacations in a cottage near Brant Lake. He and an enterprising Brant Lake Camp counselor named Arthur Schwartz collaborated on a song, Hart writing the words, Schwartz the music, about a camper who would rather read than play softball or swim. They called it "I Love to Lie Awake in Bed," though you may know it as "I Guess I'll Have to Change My Plan," with new lyrics from Howard Dietz, another Columbia man. Fred Astaire and Jack Buchanan sing it in The Band Wagon. But when Schwartz originally wrote the song, Lorenz Hart's lyric extolled the virtues of summer camp. Lying awake late at night, the camper in his bunk conjures up the canopy of stars overhead and slides into sleep with a sweet look of contentment on his face. Absent are the daring puns and jests of the lyricist's mature work, but the internal rhymes and half-rhymes ("taps" and "flaps," "born" and "corner") are *echt* Lorenz Hart, and the tune and words became the official Brant Lake Camp anthem. As for "I Guess I'll Have to Change My Plan," Dietz's insouciant confession of unrequited love ("Why did I buy those blue pajamas?") suits Schwartz's music splendidly. I recommend Mel Tormé's cover—and the piano version in the background of a scene between Humphrey Bogart and Lauren Bacall in The Big Sleep (1946). The scene involves a change of plan, not of heart, so the piano player can segue amiably into "Blue Room," an ode to nuptial bliss. Forties flicks and jazz standards were made for each other.

If I were writing a Shavian play in which music and lyrics compete over which one is more important, this would be the moment to call Dorothy Hammerstein to the stand. Dorothy has been deposed saying that everyone thinks Jerome Kern wrote "Ol' Man River," but what Kern wrote was—and here she hums the tune—while her husband wrote "Ol' Man River." (Score one for the lyricists and for spousal loyalty.) I'm not sure how Shaw would present the information that Dick's father, an obstetrician, had delivered Oscar's two oldest children (both from his first marriage). But I know that the character I play says "Small world, isn't it?" I, a writer, can always be counted on to argue in favor of Lorenz Hart's wit and Dorothy Fields's charm and Yip Harburg's dash and Gus Kahn's sprightly intelligence. But in my mind the realms of words and music are separate. The lyricists played on a field of talent, the composers on a field of genius.

From Hammerstein, I learned about the dissolute end of Larry Hart, incredibly clever and uniquely sad, who tossed off polysyllabic rhymes like "Yonkers" and "conquers," "Crusoe" and "trousseau," or "I'll sing to him" and "worship the trousers that cling to him," in "Manhattan" and "Blue Room" and "Bewitched, Bothered, and Bewildered." He was a dynamo, Hammerstein said. We worked on the Columbia varsity show with Herman Mankiewicz, who went on to write the screenplay for *Citizen Kane*. Some people think he deserved even more credit for that picture than its director, Orson Welles. But Larry. (Hammerstein shook his head.) Larry was, to put it bluntly, a tormented homosexual. He was barely five feet tall and had a head too big for his body. Did Dick Rodgers ever refer to him in disgust as "that little fag"? Probably. Times and vocabulary were different then, and Dick did put up with a lot. Dick said that there was a "statute of limitations" on gratitude. But there was also the time when a trade publisher approached him at a party and asked him if it was true that Larry was "a fairy." Dick grabbed him by the coat collar and said, "I've never heard that. And if you print it, I'll kill you."[4] Poor Larry. He had a much faster wit than I, said Oscar, ever the gallant man. There was no comparison, he said. Larry was sophisticated in his rhymes and quick with a pun—and not the kind you groan at. He came from a middle-class home and lived with his mother, who always wanted him to get married, so he suffered endless guilt from having what you fellows today call "sexual ambivalence," and what else do they say? Low self esteem? Yes, he didn't much like being by himself. A drinking problem? And how. He couldn't handle it. It got to the point where a single beer would do him in. And through it all he was the soul of generosity. A little guy, always in motion. I once called him an "electrified gnome." You should have seen him skipping and dancing around the stage. He never sat still. To get him to write the lyrics for a song Dick had to find him first, and then he just about had to lock him in the room. "In all the time I knew him, I never saw him walk slowly," Oscar said in his slow, thoughtful way. "I never saw his face in repose. I never heard him chuckle quietly. He laughed loudly at other people's jokes and at his own, too.

His large eyes danced, and his head would wag." Well, Oscar was undoubtedly the finest eulogist of the lyricists.[5]

In 1943, Hammerstein agreed to write *Oklahoma!* with Rodgers but only after Larry had definitively declined in every sense of that dismal word. Hart was too unstable or too drunk to work with, and yet Rodgers said he cried when he left Larry at his apartment on the day he said no to *Oklahoma!* "You know, Dick, I've really never understood why you've put up with me all these years," Larry said. "It's been crazy. The best thing for you to do is forget about me." Larry had written the words for all the tunes Rodgers had crafted on the piano, "My Romance" and "Where or When," "Falling in Love with Love," "The Lady Is a Tramp," "There's a Small Hotel," and "I Could Write a Book." But Larry had rejected the idea of adapting Lynn Riggs's 1931 play *Green Grow the Lilacs* to the musical stage. So Dick asked Oscar. Many thought that Hammerstein was washed up at the time, and Rodgers's decision to work with him raised eyebrows. In the 1930s, Hammerstein's shows failed at precisely the same time that Rodgers and Hart had gone from strength to strength. In retrospect, however, the decision to replace Hart with Hammerstein seems if anything overdetermined. Rodgers was, consciously or not, reverting to the primal moment of his vocation, the night his older brother took him to see the Columbia varsity show and he met the tall, courtly Hammerstein backstage. Moreover, Hammerstein had done his best work in partnership with Jerome Kern, the composer Rodgers had revered from his teenage years. Teaming up with Hammerstein would give him a chance to surpass Kern, and it is tempting, whether or not you subscribe to Harold Bloom's theory of influence anxiety, to consider that Rodgers and Hammerstein's *South Pacific* is competing with Kern and Hammerstein's *Show Boat* as America's greatest operetta. You can't tell me that when Rodgers wrote "Shall We Dance?" for *The King and I* he was unaware that the Gershwins had written a song with the same title and that it was possible that the new song was the finer piece of work.

Advance word had it that the first Rodgers and Hammerstein musical would flop. No gags, no girls, no chance, said the columnists. (Or maybe it was: no legs, no jokes, no chance.) The show came together at the last minute, and when the curtain went up on Curly singing "Oh, What a Beautiful Mornin'," I like to think that at least some of the first-nighters knew they were witnessing a major event. If the history of the Broadway musical is considered as a progression toward the full integration of story and song, where the music and lyrics must pertain to the dramatic situation and must suit the character,[6] *Oklahoma!* marked the point of no return. And if anyone was in a position to know just how revolutionary the moment was, it was Larry Hart, Rodgers's partner on *Babes in Arms* and *A Connecticut Yankee* and *Jumbo* and *The Boys from Syracuse*. Imagine what Larry felt like when *Oklahoma!* opened on March 31, 1943. There he sat with his mother and understood exactly what Dick had accomplished without him. At a victory party later that night, Larry ran up to Dick, threw his arms around him, and declared the show would run forever. It was a brave and affectionate gesture. Within a month Hart's mother was dead. Later that year on a cold November night Hart got falling-down drunk, started babbling incoherently, and had to be ushered out of the theater. He was discovered shortly thereafter sitting on the curb of a city street with no overcoat in the rain, suffering from pneumonia. He died on November 22, 1943.

Be Careful, It's My Heart

Based on short stories by John O'Hara, *Pal Joey*, the last of the Rodgers and Hart musicals, was arguably a daring advance for the genre in December 1940. Rodgers called it "the most satisfying and mature work" he had done with Hart. With Gene Kelly in the lead and showstoppers on the order of "Bewitched, Bothered, and Bewildered," the show had a respectable first run, was successfully revived in 1952, and was made into a movie with Frank Sinatra, Kim Novak, and Rita Hayworth five years later. But on opening night, Rodgers observed, half the audience cheered and the other half looked shell-shocked. In retrospect it was perhaps too risky to center a musical on a villainous main character. The unkindest cut came from the pen of *The New York Times*'s Brooks Atkinson. In one of the most famous last lines in the history of theater reviews, Atkinson wrote, "Although *Pal Joey* is expertly done, can you draw sweet water from a foul well?" Hart was wounded to the quick. Gene Kelly was with him when the review came out. "He broke down, cried, sobbed, because he wanted Atkinson, for whatever reasons, to say this show was a milestone. He locked himself in his bedroom and wouldn't come out."[7]

Asked by an anthologist to pick the first poem she loved that made her want to be a poet, Eleanor Wilner named Hart's lyric "The Lady Is a Tramp." "The great song lyricists were my first poets, and musical comedy was my text," she wrote. "Not only was I, like millions of others, entranced by the language, the clever rhymes, the delightful melodies, and the dramatic voices, but here was my first exposure as well to poetic truth as opposed to conventional pieties." With its lyric defying the tyranny of snobbism— the lady is a tramp because she stays awake at the opera, arrives at the theater on time, and can have a grand time in the humble precincts of Coney Island, the lake in Central Park, or the bleachers at the Polo Grounds—Rodgers and Hart's "The Lady Is a Tramp" became, she added, her "personal credo."[8] Nor is Wilner the only poet to have been affected in her poetic practice by Hart. Brad Leithauser recently published a pair of poems in homage to Hart and in the lyricist's style. The speaker of Leithauser's "A Good List" tells us he "never practiced arson, even as a prank, / Brightened church-suppers with off-color jokes, / Concocted an archeological hoax— / Or dumped bleach in a goldfish tank."[9]

Ardent advocacy of Hart does not, however, require us to make the case for his songs as poems or to analyze his lyrics in the manner of a New Critic treating the poems of John Donne. I agree with Alec Wilder as paraphrased by his editor, James Maher: "Song lyrics, the author feels, are not poems and are not meant to be, and to discuss them as poetry is to invent a pretense that is an embarrassing burden to the truly professional lyricist."[10] The point is not that

Hart was a poet, though I would not begrudge him the honorific. The point is that as a lyricist, arguably a more demanding vocation, this brilliant, carousing, unhappy little man—rejected for military duty because he wasn't tall enough—was a nonpareil.

I recently heard Sheldon Harnick (*Fiddler on the Roof, She Loves Me*) single out Hart's "Falling in Love with Love" for the systematic internal rhyme between the fourth and sixth notes in lines five, seven, and eleven to echo the identity of "love" and "love" in the title and first line of the song. Talk about cleverness! Only Ira Gershwin and Cole Porter can give him a run for the money on the cleverness front. And Hart used his ready wit not to relieve the sadness but to reveal it. In "It Never Entered My Mind," the singer wishes his lover were there to "get into my hair again," in both the idiomatic and the salacious senses. Because it kids itself, Hart's depiction of the abandoned lover, "uneasy in [his] easy chair," ordering "orange juice for one," is far more moving than any number of heart-on-sleeve ballads. And then there is the lyricist's effort to persuade himself that he is "Glad to Be Unhappy." It may be a losing battle; Hart always leads with his chin. But listen to Billie Holiday sing that song on *Lady in Satin*.

A Cockeyed Optimist

If folks adored Hart, they revered Hammerstein, a real mensch, who never forgot that failure was a possibility. After *Oklahoma!* made its triumphant debut in 1943, Hammerstein took out a full-page ad in *Variety* acknowledging that "I've Done It Before And I Can Do It Again!"—and by "it" he meant "flopped": He humbly recalled the list of honorable failures he had had in the previous decade. In many ways the partnership Rodgers had with Hammerstein inverted the one he'd had with Hart. In photographs, Hammerstein, whose theatrical lineage went back two generations, towers over Rodgers just as Rodgers had formerly towered over Hart; at five feet seven the composer was seven inches taller than his first partner and eight shorter than his second. Hammerstein wrote the lyrics and presented them to Dick, who then set them to music—the exact opposite of how Rodgers worked with Hart. Once you know this fact, you immediately understand why the music Rodgers wrote with one partner differs so sharply from the music he wrote with the other. Oscar was a librettist before he was anything else. He led Rodgers with his lyrics and in the core belief that the play was the thing: The songs were to serve the specific demands of a serious plot, a coherent love story with inevitable complications in cowboy country, or at a fishing village in Maine, or on a South Pacific island during World War II. It may be because of Hammerstein's contributions that the best Rodgers and Hammerstein musicals are superior to just about anything else ever produced on Broadway, including the musicals featuring Rodgers and Hart standards, sometimes three or four in an evening.

Of the songs they wrote together, Rodgers said that it was never the sad ones that made Oscar cry; it was songs like "The Surrey with the Fringe on Top" with its naïve romanticism. This is the same reaction I have, and it helps me understand something about the nature of happiness and its relation to tears. As romance is in the longing, not the having, so happiness, too, exists most distinctly as an absence, elusive though near, more available as a memory or a dream than as a palpable actuality. Bound up with innocence and disinclined to take note of itself, happiness is the least self-conscious of states. It may be, as Joseph Conrad writes in the concluding sentence of *Youth*, something "that while it is expected is already gone—has passed unseen, in a sigh, in a flash—together with the youth, with the strength, with the romance of illusions." Andrea Most proposes another reason why we cry at musical comedies in revival. It is not sentiment but a "sense of fullness that requires release" that causes the tears to flow. The audience consists of people who know the songs, anticipate them, and imagine themselves in the role of the singer.[11]

It has become fashionable to condescend to Hammerstein on the grounds that he wrote sugarcoated lyrics in the "poetical" manner. If excess of virtue is a defect, his generous heart led to my least favorite Rodgers and Hammerstein song, "Climb Every Mountain" in *The Sound of Music*. Pieties do not wear well, and friends of mine, lovers of popular song, cringe at the memory of being a child instructed by a cheerful governess to "Whistle a Happy Tune." Comparisons made between Hart and Hammerstein work invariably to diminish the latter. Hart's words were in witty and ironic counterpoint to the lush lyricism of Rodgers; Hammerstein's words pushed Rodgers into full-throated sentiment. Philip Furia, in *The Poets of Tin Pan Alley*, considers Hammerstein's lyric for Kern's "All the Things You Are" to consist of "sonorous paeans" that make it inferior to, say, Cole Porter's "You're the Top" in wit, cleverness, and "stylish verse." Hammerstein tries too hard to be poetic ("the breathless hush of evening") where Porter is "casually colloquial," with a "flippantly antiromantic" component undercutting the sentiment. Furia states the consensus view, and you're bound to agree if you analyze the lyrics independent from the music.[12] Nevertheless, after the German national team lost to the eventual world-cup winning team from Italy in July 2006, the song "You'll Never Walk Alone" from *Carousel* filled the arena in Germany, and I can't have been the only one present to appreciate the irony of the choice. Here in the heartland of the Holocaust, the song that lifted the spirits of the many thousands of disappointed spectators was a hymn, or as near a thing to a hymn as popular music has to offer, written by a couple of Ashkenazi Jews who lived to create such lasting works only because their prescient grandfathers had abandoned Europe and taken their families to the new world in advance of Czarist pogroms and Nazi death camps.

Hammerstein, with his thoroughly theatrical imagination, had the ability to achieve in the lyrics of a song the consummate exposition of the story of a man and a woman in love, as in the "bench" scene in *Carousel* culminating in the "If I Loved You" duet, or the polka in *The King and I*, the song Anna sings when the king consents to take dance instruction from her: "Shall We Dance?" In a collection of his lyrics Hammerstein wrote, "There are few things in life of which I am certain, but I am sure of this one thing, that the song is the servant of the play, that it is wrong to write first what you think is an attractive song and then try to wedge it into a story." This can stand as a one-sentence summary for the thesis Lehman Engel advances in his book *Words with Music* to account for the successful emergence, in the 1940s and 1950s, of unified musicals where previously shows had existed as pretexts for the singing and dancing of miscellaneous songs. Some of the songs Hammerstein wrote with Rodgers are so show-specific that they are of limited appeal out of their stage context.[13] But he also crafted the words for "It Might as Well Be Spring," which won an Academy Award and became an irresistible jazz standard, and "Ol' Man River" is in a class by itself. When Hammerstein died, the theaters went dark on Broadway and on London's West End. The lights were out all over.

The Corner Office

I got to visit Richard Rodgers in his corner office at 598 Madison Avenue one February day in my sophomore year at Columbia. Conservatively dressed in a pinstriped suit, Rodgers graciously consented to let me interview him for the *Columbia Spectator* even though Columbia had pissed him off when he proposed building a musical and theatrical complex, and Grayson Kirk, the university's president, said nothing was more boring than the arts, except maybe dentistry, as far as raising funds was concerned. Just think: Lincoln Center could have been part of Columbia.

I asked which came first, the words or the music.

Always the same question, Rodgers said indulgently. With Larry the music came first and with Oscar the lyrics did.

Was it true that Rodgers had to coerce Hart to sit still long enough to write the lyrics? Quite true, Rodgers said. You know I put all this in a book. It's called *Musical Stages*.

I quoted a passage from the book to show I had read it. You said that when you met Larry in his apartment at 59 West 119th Street you guys hit it off immediately and you left his house that day "having acquired in one afternoon a career, a partner, a best friend, and a source of permanent irritation."

He was all those things, Dick said.

When I said that my girlfriend adored George Balanchine and had a particular love for Rodgers's ballet *Slaughter on Tenth Avenue*, he looked pleased. Balanchine made it easy, he said. I knew nothing about choreography and wasn't sure how to proceed. Balanchine just said, "You write it, I do it." And that's exactly how it went. I met Balanchine through Larry. The whole ballet was Larry's idea, actually. Did you know that Balanchine called Larry the "Shelley of America"?[14]

I have to confess I was nervous at the interview. I couldn't banish from my mind what Mel Tormé said about the first time he met Richard Rodgers. Mel had a lot of respect and admiration for Rodgers, but he used an odd word to describe him. He called Rodgers "one of the most aggressive composers" America has ever produced. "Aggressive," rather than "ambitious." When Tormé was twenty-two, he had a gig at the Copacabana. *Carousel* was still going strong on

Broadway, and some nights, after his first show at the club, Mel would hop in a cab to the Majestic and catch the end of the second act of *Carousel*, which may be, just from the point of view of the music, the finest of the Rodgers and Hammerstein collaborations. And one time Mel was there standing in the back of the theater next to another man who turned out to be Richard Rodgers himself contemplating his work on the stage like Aristotle contemplating the bust of Homer. I didn't want to intrude, Mel told me. But I felt I had to say something. I said, "This is the ninth time I have seen this masterpiece of yours, Mr. Rodgers, and every time I see it I walk out of this theater in tears." You know what he said in reply? He said, "Well, when you stop crying, stop coming."[5] Mel shook his head. He felt like two cents, but what are you going to do? Rodgers was an autocrat. He wanted singers to sing his songs the way he wrote them, not as interpreted or "arranged" in a different tempo. On his weekly radio show, Jonathan Schwartz—disc jockey deluxe and keeper of the flame of "High Standards" on satellite radio—laughs recalling the time Rosemary Clooney did a swinging version of "Falling in Love with Love." Rodgers happened to be in the room, and when she walked over to him afterward, he said only, "That song is a waltz." Peggy Lee recorded "Lover," another evergreen Rodgers and Hart waltz. Asked for his opinion, Rodgers deadpanned: "I don't know why Peggy picked on me when she could have fucked up 'Silent Night.' "[16]

I asked Rodgers where his musical ideas came from.

Here, let me show you something, Rodgers said, striding over to the piano. He began playing "It Might as Well Be Spring." Rodgers looked at me. "Remind me how the lyric goes," he said. I quoted it: "I'm as restless as a willow in a wind storm. / I'm as jumpy as a puppet on a string." Rodgers grew animated. Listen, he said, and played a succession of notes. Do you see how the tune jumps up and down like a puppet? That gave me the theme for the whole song.

"My favorite Hammerstein lyric," I volunteered. "It won you guys the Academy Award." I also explained that in music humanities, which all Columbia sophomores had to take, I was writing a paper for Mr. Chusid on the frequency and context in which the word "heart" turns up in Rodgers and Hart songs.

Rodgers smiled a bit wanly. Have you reached any conclusions? he asked.

Well, I said, it's the final word of your waltz "Lover." "Lover, I surrender to my heart." And then there's "With a Song in My Heart."

That's when Rodgers described the origin of "My Heart Stood Still." We were getting out of a cab in Paris and another cab almost sideswiped us and one of the girls we were escorting back to their hotel cried, "Oh, my heart stood still!" Larry said that would make a great title for a song and so I wrote it down in my little black address book. And that would have been the end of it, except that one morning I was looking for a phone number and I came across a page with the words "My Heart Stood Still." Then I remembered Paris, and it was early and Larry was still asleep. So I simply sat down at the piano and wrote a melody for a man whose intensity of emotion would overwhelm his heart. When Larry woke up, I played it for him. He wrote the lyric in no time at all.[17]

Speaking of speed, I said, is it true you wrote "Bali Ha'i" between courses while having dinner with Hammerstein and the play's director, Joshua Logan?

Rodgers coughed. People don't realize how much thinking you have to do ahead of time, he said. Months. You've got to take that into account. There's a difference between "flying time" and "elapsed time." Let's say it took me about five hours to write the score of *Oklahoma!* Okay, that would be the "flying time." But a song almost never occurs to me spontaneously. Weeks and months of planning and thinking precede the actual composition.[18] And here, Rodgers looked at his watch. I thanked him. He was a courteous man, though a cold fish. Even Hammerstein said that Rodgers would have made a "wonderful surgeon."[19] Five hours, I thought. The whole score of *Oklahoma!*

No one seemed to like Rodgers very much. He drank and bedded the young babes in the cast, said one survivor of that long ago and faraway time. He behaved like a banker or a CEO, said another. Okay, but how many neurotic workaholics have written shows as marvelous and songs as deathless as Richard Rodgers? For thirty glorious minutes a day he communed with his muse. So his daughter explains. "A morning person, an enviably quick study, and cheerfully businesslike about his work, he'd go to the piano at nine and was usually through by nine-thirty," Mary Rodgers writes.[20] He must have lived for those precious thirty minutes. And one fine night Mary Martin flew in through the window like the ghost of Peter Pan and gushed into happy talk about Mr. Rodgers. She said that Jerry Kern was considered difficult and demanding, uncompromising, and dismissive of the singer who was not equal to the vast vocal range required by one of his songs. In this department Dick Rodgers, as committed to the musical theater as his master, was very different. Aware of my limited range, she said, he wrote songs that made me look great in *South Pacific*, and he and Oscar took my suggestions to heart. You know it was I who came up with the idea of the oversized sailor suit I wore during my "Honeybun" number and they used that image on posters for the show.

I nodded my head. I did know that. I said that my father and mother always told me that she was the perfect vehicle for Oscar Hammerstein's corny-as-Kansas love of America. I said this, and she smiled. You know something? They were all envious of Dick. Probably no one wrote faster than he did. He composed with such speed as to scandalize any lyricist. Hammerstein agonized for weeks over "Oh, What a Beautiful Morning," the first song they wrote together. He spent a week mulling over the first word of the chorus: should it be "Oh, what a beautiful mornin' " or just "What a beautiful mornin'.'" When he was finally satisfied with the lyric, Oscar brought it to Dick, who looked it over, nodded his head, walked over to the piano and wrote the tune that Curly sings at the beginning of *Oklahoma!* That's not just speed. That's genius.

We'll Have Manhattan

In 1938 *Time* magazine put Rodgers and Hart on the cover and called them "the boys from Columbia." According to

Time, Rodgers supplied the method, Hart the madness. "Trim, affluent-looking" Rodgers, who "seems to be the businessman of the pair," lives with his family on swanky East 77th Street. Hart, residing with his mother on Central Park West, "scowls at white ties, gives manners-be-damned, whiskey-by-the-case, all-night free-for-alls," and has to be "yanked out of bed" late in the day and kept on a leash. They met in 1919 "when Hart was 23 and just out of Columbia, and Rodgers 16 and just going in."

As a senior in high school I applied to Columbia and made it my first choice in part because the Columbia Varsity Show had this mythical importance in the life of Richard Rodgers. I wanted to go to Columbia more than anything in the world, not only because of the talent and intelligence I expected to find there but because if you went to Columbia, you had all of New York as your playground. If you had offered me a car, a flat of my own, and a small independent income to go somewhere else, I'd have turned it all down to go to Columbia, scholarship or no scholarship.

By the time I entered college, New York, New York was musically defined by Leonard Bernstein and choreographed by Jerome Robbins. It was smart-ass central, "Where no one lives on account of the pace, / But seven million are screaming for space" (as Betty Comden and Adolph Green put it in *On the Town*). And in the slums the whites and the Puerto Ricans held gang fights that resembled dancing of the most acrobatic and passionate kind, even if the end result was a knife in the gut. I like to be in America, and that means the island Manhattan. "Smoke on your pipe and put that in!" (as Stephen Sondheim put it in *West Side Story*). Get cool, man.

Every street was a boulevard of broken dreams, but love was always just around the corner. It could happen to you. And you could live there cheaply and it was the capital of show business, of culture and of commerce, and the capital of Judaism as well. Once, years later, when I shared a taxi with Woody Allen, we crossed the Triborough Bridge and the view was so breathtaking that Woody almost took his eyes off the meter. The whole time there were Gershwin songs in the background, like "Do, Do, Do" and "He Loves and She Loves" and "Love Is Here to Stay." According to the Gershwin brothers, the key to happiness was my gal, my song, and my Lord. That made sense. The pursuit of happiness was the American dream, one part of it anyway, and not an insignificant one. And this was the best place to look for it. If you could make it here you could make it anywhere. The city was a wondrous toy, just made for a girl and boy. Who could ask for anything more?

New York City, the musical: a dozen showstoppers plus a few extras for curtain calls. May I list a few? The opening of Bernstein's *On the Town*: New York, New York, a helluva town, and wasn't it something that in the movie version Comden and Green felt they had to substitute "wonderful" for "helluva"? How about the Burton Lane and Ralph Freed standard "How About You?"—a charming list song that begins "I like New York in June" and compliments Franklin Roosevelt's looks. The Gershwins' "They All Laughed" qualifies as a New York song because it names Rockefeller Center as an unlikely success story, though it's hard to believe that this midtown fixture ever needed to overcome the doubts of skeptics. From *Porgy and Bess* I'd opt for

"There's a Boat That's Leaving Soon for New York" as performed by Sammy Davis, Jr., in the role of Sportin' Life. (Poor Sammy: the one member of Sinatra's Rat Pack who managed to be black, Jewish, and blind in one eye. When a mob kingpin got pissed off at Sinatra, one of his henchmen offered not only to eliminate the singer but to "poke out the one-eyed black gentleman's other eye"—only he didn't say "black gentleman." On November 25, 1987, the Associated Press reported that "the 62-year-old actor-singer-dancer" would undergo surgery at Cedars Sinai Medical Center "to restore a hip reconstructed two years ago." Wire service headline: "Sammy Davis to Get Hip.") "Autumn in New York" by Vernon Duke, a.k.a. Vladimir Dukelsky, most definitely has a place in the anthology album I seem unconsciously to be creating in this paragraph. We can use the Sinatra version of "How About You?" with its extraordinary conclusion—it's on his *Songs for Swinging Lovers* album—and Bing Crosby's "They All Laughed," which he recorded with Bunny Berrigan in the same year, 1956. From Frank Loesser's *Guys and Dolls*, the consummate Broadway show, I've got to have "The Oldest Established Permanent Floating Crap Game in New York" from the original theatrical or movie sound track. For "Autumn in New York" I'm tempted to go with an all-instrumental version; Bud Powell on piano (1954) and Charlie Parker on alto sax (1952) are two that come to mind. Duke wrote the words as well as the sublime music. The lyrics are okay but not nearly as good as Yip Harburg's for the same composer's "April in Paris," an even better song.

At least one tune on the record will be new to most listeners. It was written specifically for Sinatra to sing at one of his stints at the Copa. "Meet Me at the Copa" has music by Axel Stordahl, Sinatra's arranger from the time he left the Tommy Dorsey band to strike out on his own, and a Sammy Cahn lyric. It dates to September 21, 1950, ebb tide in Sinatra's career. His popularity had gone down because of his gangster connections, because he had lost his temper and punched out an antagonistic newspaper columnist, and most of all because he had abandoned his wife and young family in favor of Ava Gardner, who was as bewitching as the young Elizabeth Taylor and even more dangerous. Less than five months earlier Sinatra's voice gave out during his third set at the Copa one spring night. Skitch Henderson, who was leading the band, remembers that "he opened his mouth to sing after the band introduction, and nothing came out. Not a sound. . . . It became so quiet, so intensely quiet in the club—they were like watching a man walk off a cliff." Sinatra had suffered a submucosal hemorrhage of the throat and was ordered to keep his mouth shut.[22] The critics were less than kind. The *Herald-Tribune* wrote, "Vocally, there isn't quite the same old black magic there used to be when Mr. Sinatra wrenched 'Night and Day' from his sapling frame and thousands swooned." Still, I'd give anything to transport myself to 10 East 60th Street to catch Sinatra's act when he introduced "Meet Me at the Copa." The Cahn lyric refers to folks who like to go to the art museum,

> *And out in Brooklyn there's a ballpark and a team,*
> *But I don't care a whole lot if I never see 'em.*

And why? Because of the lure of the legendary nightspot. That old Brooklyn ballpark and team have gone the way of the Copa itself, but the song lives on in *Swing and Dance with Frank Sinatra*, a must-have CD from the Columbia period, with arrangements by George Siravo.

Duke Ellington will play his theme song, "Take the A Train," to kick off what I persist in regarding as "side two" of the album. I wonder if there's a recording with Jerry Orbach doing "Lullaby of Broadway" (music Harry Warren, lyrics Al Dubin). I'm pretty sure I saw him do "Forty-second Street" by the same songwriters. For "Lullaby of Birdland" (music George Shearing, words George Davis Weiss), I'll go with Mel Tormé. I'm undecided between Lee Wiley's wistful and Ella Fitzgerald's exuberant version of "Manhattan," Rodgers and Hart's breakout song of 1925. It was their first hit after years of trying, and they were still young (Rodgers was twenty-three and Hart was thirty). I remember the first time I heard it. For some reason I thought the first line was not "We'll have Manhattan" but "I'll take Manhattan," and I assumed it referred to a customer's request for a cocktail made of rye whiskey and sweet vermouth with a maraschino cherry tossed in for good luck. I used to walk through Chinatown or Little Italy with Hart's lyrics on my brain. "And tell me what street / Compares with Mott Street" on a July day. Why would anyone want to live anywhere else but this city where the *you* of your dreams would feel so "rich in" two rooms and kitchen? Lorenz Hart: Thou swell, thou witty, thou grand. Wide awake he could make his most fantastic dreams come true, if only on paper. Anyone can rhyme "pain" and "Spain." (Listen to "Autumn in New York.") But only Lorenz Hart would rhyme a "castle rising in Spain" and a "constantly surprising refrain," as he does in "My Romance."

I would insist on "Manhattan Serenade" (music Louis Alter, lyrics Harold Adamson) as Jo Stafford sang it, endowing a bicycle metaphor with romantic glamour: "Our kiss was a sky ride to the highest stars. / We made it without touching the handlebars." (The instrumental lead-in to Stafford's version of the song, cool horns and warm strings, is what you hear in part I of *The Godfather* as a plane streaks across the sky transporting *consigliere* Tom Hagen from New York to Los Angeles where he will help down-and-out singer Johnny Fontaine get the film part that will revive his career.) Jimmy Cagney would walk and talk his way through George M. Cohan's "Give My Regards to Broadway," and Judy Garland and Fred Astaire would sing "Easter Parade" if only for Irving Berlin's rich couplet about how the photographers on Fifth Avenue will snap us, "And you'll find that you're / In the rotogravure." I would definitely include the final number on Sinatra's *Come Fly With Me* album, a Sammy Cahn and James Van Heusen collaboration called "It's Nice to Be Traveling," which radiates a joyful winking New York chauvinism. The senoritas and the mädchens, though comely, do not have "What the models have / On Madison Ave." Great as it is to travel, it's even better to come home, and "your fate is / Where the Empire State is." (The song plays over the closing credits of the Kurt Russell–Halle Berry thriller *Executive Decision*.) My Manhattan album culminates in the great big "New York, New York" (music John Kander, lyrics Fred Ebb) as Sinatra did it with that long expressive "and" that precedes "if I can make it there" at the end of the song. It has become the city's official anthem, and its performance by an opera singer makes the Belmont stakes in June not only the longest and last of the three "triple crown" races for three-year-old thoroughbreds but a musically superior event.

As with cities, whole decades have their ideal playlists. Dorothy Fields would have a box seat in the theater of my heart if she had done nothing else but write the words for Jimmy McHugh's music in "On the Sunny Side of the Street." A true Depression-era song, it would anchor my list of songs from the 1930s, in this order:

1. Fred Astaire, "Let's Face the Music and Dance," music and lyrics by Irving Berlin
2. Ginger Rogers, "The Gold-Diggers' Song (We're in the Money)," music Harry Warren, lyrics Al Dubin
3. Bing Crosby, "Pennies from Heaven," music Arthur Johnston, lyrics Johnny Burke
4. Lee Wiley trembling and throaty with "The Street of Dreams," music Victor Young, lyrics Sam M. Lewis
5. Bing Crosby again, "Brother, Can You Spare a Dime?" music Jay Gorney, lyrics Yip Harburg
6. Louis Armstrong, "I Gotta Right to Sing the Blues," music Harold Arlen, lyrics Ted Koehler
7. Nat King Cole or maybe Rosemary Clooney or Maxine Sullivan, "My Blue Heaven," music Walter Donaldson, lyrics George White
8. Barbra Streisand, "Happy Days Are Here Again," music Milton Ager, lyrics Jack Yellen (FDR's campaign song in 1932)

9. Judy Garland, "Get Happy," music Harold Arlen, lyrics Ted Koehler

10. Barbra Streisand, "Happy Days Are Here Again" and Judy Garland, "Get Happy," sung as a medley

11. Lena Horne, "Stormy Weather," music Harold Arlen, lyrics Ted Koehler

12. Sinatra's 1954 cover of "Wrap Your Troubles in Dreams," music Harry Barris, lyrics by Koehler with Billy Moll

13. Ella Fitzgerald or possibly the Art Tatum piano instrumental, "Paper Moon," music Harold Arlen, lyrics Yip Harburg

14. Sarah Vaughan, "I Can't Give You Anything But Love, Baby," music Jimmy McHugh, lyrics Dorothy Fields

15. Judy Garland again, "Over the Rainbow," music Harold Arlen, lyrics Yip Harburg

16. Judy Garland and the gang on the yellow brick road and the quest to see the wizard, music Harold Arlen, lyrics Yip Harburg

17. Tommy Dorsey orchestra with girl chorus, "On the Sunny Side of the Street," music Jimmy McHugh, lyrics Dorothy Fields

What a fine story those songs would tell. About a fellow who has the right to feel lowdown and sings about it down around the river, and the song itself lifts his spirits, and one fine day he's going to get happy, look skyward, and walk in the sun once more. It doesn't surprise me that the only composer with more than one title on the list is Arlen, who has six, three with Harburg and three with Koehler, because—as Steve Blier put it, explaining Judy Garland's attraction to Arlen's dark, intricate, bluesy songs—"Putting a good face on the pain is what both of them were about."[23] An Arlen song in Garland's voice made for "good Jewish music," in Kern's phrase.

The best of the Depression-era songs exemplify W. H. Auden's category of "escape-art," which Auden defends on the grounds that "man needs escape as he needs food and deep sleep."[24] Looking over the list, I am struck by the blend of melancholy and resolute good cheer in the music—and by the balance the lyrics strike between escapism and realism. On the one side, the songs dwell in the realm of fantasy and daydream: a make-believe romance, a trip to the land of Oz, or the wish fulfillment of being "in the money" or maybe just a cozy room with Molly ("and Baby makes three"). On the other side, the songs are old-fashioned pep talks with a new urgency. They counsel bravery, a sense of humor, and a positive outlook in the teeth of misfortune—but they do acknowledge the misfortune. Above all, the songs emphasize the transformative power of the imagination: Raindrops are pennies if you think they are, though there's no denying the inclemency of the weather or the urgent need for coins of even the lowest denomination. "Pennies from Heaven" is the song that Dennis Potter marked as definitive of the period— it is the title he gave to his multipart television series (and, later, movie) about a traveling sheet-music salesman in those desperate days. The theme of the song is the tried-and-true one of April showers and May flowers bent splendidly out of shape by the monetary imagery. The fantasy of easy money, the wish gratified instantly with no effort on the dreamer's part, the coins falling like manna from the heavens—how wonderfully, weirdly American—and yet how melancholy the melody as Bing sings it. Others would insist that the anthem of the Great Depression is Yip Harburg's "Brother, Can You Spare a Dime?" and certainly the voice of Bing Crosby in that song is the voice of the American worker, now beggar, in the bitterness of his predicament. Unemployed, friendless, he waits in a breadline, feeling mystified and betrayed. The greatest pathos is in these lines: "Say, don't you remember? / They called me 'Al,' / It was 'Al' all the time." The song is sincere, heroic, and more effective politically than a thousand editorials. Nevertheless, my vote goes to the girls of the Tommy Dorsey Orchestra harmonizing happily on the side of the street that's sunny. The song is about you, dear listener. Your worry may not go away, but it's time to leave it on the doorstep, don coat and hat, and venture forth. In the bridge, where we move from the second-person to the first-person point of view, the key line is "Now I'm not afraid." In this realm where attitude is everything, happiness is not contingent on pennies, a dime, or "the money." Without a cent you, too, can be "as rich as Rockefeller."

By my reckoning, Jewish songwriters figure in the composition of all but two or three of the sixteen Depression-era songs on my playlist. And this to me makes perfect sense. These songs about American promise and optimism, evoking the vision of the founding fathers, exist in precise opposition to the suicidal darkness and fog of prejudice that swept over Europe in the 1930s, the "dishonest decade," as Auden designated it in his poem "September 1, 1939."

VI

The World on a String

Got the string around my finger.

TED KOEHLER, "I've Got the World on a String"

I Got Plenty of Chutzpah

A display of chutzpah, for which Yeshiva boys get punished, was a necessary ingredient for the life of a Jewish genius. Shortly after George Gershwin's death in 1937, Jerome Kern recollected something George had said to him long after achieving success in the recital hall as well as on Broadway: " 'Do you think,' he asked with naïveté, 'that now I am capable of grand opera? Because, you know,' he continued, 'all I've got is a lot of talent and plenty of *chutzpah*.' It was then," Kern concluded, "that these ears realized that they were listening to a man touched with genius."[1] The remark Jerry Kern found so endearing is echoed in Porgy's proud boast—in the opera Gershwin went on to write—that he has "plenty o' nuttin" and that this is all that he needs. "Chutzpah" as Gershwin used it means something like bravado or gumption, not arrogance but supreme self-confidence combined with charm. Gershwin knew himself to be one who would always be indulged or forgiven: He was, in his brother Ira's words, too "vibrant, dynamic, honest and charming" to dislike.[2] He was also too innocent and uncalculating in the assertion of his preeminence. He justified his chutzpah in action accompanied with panache. And truly he was the most singular of the lot. Not only could he write stand-alone songs, he could write for the theater; he could cross over the classical divide and write preludes and rhapsodies, and he could perform the piano parts of his symphonic compositions with gusto. In Irving Berlin's opinion, Gershwin alone among his contemporaries earned the right to be called a "composer" rather than the more prosaic "songwriter."

If a musical composition is the expression of the author's personality, you would have to say that Gershwin's personality combined warmth with excitement, wit, and a heavy dash of unadulterated chutzpah. When orchestra leader Paul Whiteman, self-proclaimed "King of Jazz," asked Gershwin if he would compose an orchestral piece of substance and length for a February concert he was planning, Gershwin said yes but promptly forgot about it until one afternoon, more than a month later, when his brother Ira interrupted him at a game of billiards. There was, Ira said, a story in the day's *New York Herald-Tribune:* "George Gershwin is at work on a jazz concerto." That was on January 4, 1923. Three days later George began writing. According to one account, he finished the score in eighteen days. In 1926, Gershwin shortened that further. He said he wrote the piece that came to be called *Rhapsody in Blue* "in ten days" in part to prove that "jazz is an idiom not to be limited to a mere song and chorus that consumed three minutes in presentation. The *Rhapsody* was a longer work. It required fifteen minutes for the playing." The implicit ratio (ten days of composition for a fifteen-minute piece) suggests that two days is ample time to compose a three-minute song.[3] *Rhapsody in Blue*, he said, "oozed out of my fingers." And it was Gershwin himself on the piano bench when the piece debuted on the afternoon of February 12. "Had Gershwin been more retiring, more modest, and less accomplished at the keyboard, there would probably have been no *Rhapsody in Blue for Jazz Band and Piano*," William G. Hyland observes in his study of the songwriters. "It was the unbounded confidence of this brash young twenty-five-year-old song-plugger that made the *Rhapsody* a true innovation in American music."[4]

Chutzpah as unbounded confidence, the feeling that one can do almost anything and do it well and in style: When Gershwin took up painting, an artist friend questioned the decision. "Of course I can paint!" George replied. "If you have talent you can do anything. I have a lot of talent."[5] The antics of heavyweight champion Muhammad Ali, self-proclaimed "the greatest," exemplified chutzpah at its most baroque when, out of the ring, he traded verses with Marianne Moore at a café while George Plimpton recorded what was said. Jonathan Schwartz, disc jockey nonpareil, who has done as much as anyone else to keep the music alive in a new century, provides a handy example of chutzpah that one may come to regret: the absence of *derekh eretz*. In his memoir *All in Good Time*, Schwartz recalls the party he attended as a teen when he was invited to the piano to accompany no less an eminence than Bing Crosby. Crosby named a song and a key, B-flat, and the lad replied, "How about C? You can get up there, it's not too high." By the time the music reached the release, Crosby had stopped singing, and the piano player wondered why, after all his arpeggios and flourishes ("I was swingin', I was movin', I was kickin' ass"), he received only polite and muted applause from the partygoers. Then Gene Kelly began to sing Kern's "Long Ago and Far Away," accompanied by Jonathan's father, the composer Arthur Schwartz, whose songs include "Dancing in the Dark" and "That's Entertainment."[6]

In a lecture he gave at the temple when I was a boy, the composer and music critic Kurt List talked about Gershwin from the point of view of "serious music," and Gershwin's brand of chutzpah was one of the first things he brought up. The composer bought a textbook on musical forms only after he accepted a commission to write a piano concerto. "Judging from the finished product, he might just as well have read the book after he wrote the work," Mr. List added tartly. Despite his disapproval, which I think he exaggerated for dramatic effect, it was easy even then to see how this "textbook" example could illustrate the value of chutzpah as a creative force; it required only that you regard Gershwin's deviation from convention not as a fault but as a virtue and that you deem his self-confidence warranted. Mr. List read us the article he had just completed for *Commentary* about how Gershwin, "the son of Russian-Jewish immigrants," had come to be "seen merely as a prototype of the American success story." That *merely* spoke volumes. According to Mr. List, Gershwin was "the greatest American composer—alas!"[7] Then again, if Gershwin instinctively knew what the public wanted, it was because he "was the public—one of the mass of eager young people who drew their inspiration from the lives and careers of Henry Ford and Greta Garbo."[8] Of course it didn't hurt that Gershwin also had "rare musical talent" and "exquisite harmonic subtlety" in addition to the ability to "feel accurately the pulse of popular music in the nation."

I hear an element of chutzpah in the impish or comic sense when Lorenz Hart, in "Manhattan" (music Richard Rodgers), rhymes "spoil" with "boy and goil," or when Howard Dietz, in "Rhode Island Is Famous for You" (music Arthur Schwartz), says that the state of "Wyomink" is famous for furs. Am I wrong to interpret the ostentatious cleverness of a Hart, a Dietz, or an Ira Gershwin as versions of chutzpah? Consider the snappy rhyme cheerfully at odds with the stated feeling in this buoyant couplet from Ira's "Isn't It a Pity?"

> *My nights were sour*
> *Spent with Schopenhauer*

Or the irrepressible, self-lacerating humor that enters Lorenz Hart's "It Never Entered My Mind," a sad lyric, and makes it more poignant:

> *You have what I lack myself,*
> *And now I even have to scratch my back myself.*

Or, in "That's Entertainment," Howard Dietz's cheeky summary of *Hamlet*. The play's the thing wherein

> . . . *a ghost and a prince meet,*
> *And ev'ryone ends as mincemeat.*

As to chutzpah in the strong sense of nerve or gall, especially in the service of genius, talent, and Emersonian self-reliance, think of the chutzpah required for an urban Jew (or a pair of such) to define, in song, the western frontier ("territory folks should stick together"), the ceaseless Mississippi (a "strong brown god," T. S. Eliot called it, but Oscar Hammerstein's personification of the river as an ageless man is the more memorable), the cornfields of Kansas ("as normal as blueberry pie"), and the yellow brick road leading to Oz, the enchanted land at the end of the rainbow, on the other side of the Great Depression. It took a lot of chutzpah to represent operatically the lives of poor Southern blacks in the fictional Catfish Row in Charleston, South Carolina, and almost as much to speak for the average Joe in the barracks who's in the army now and just wants a good night's rest. These are some of the stunts performed by fellows named Arlen, Berlin, Gershwin, Hammerstein, Harburg, Kern, and Rodgers. They and their confreres also extolled the virtues of various all-American girls named Amy, Dolores, Laura, Linda, Liza, Maria, Nancy, and Rosemary, contrived scores of new ways to say I love you, and managed, in one celebrated case, to articulate the meaning of Christmas and Easter, the apotheosis of show business, and the essence of the American patriotic ideal.

When I was sixteen, I heard Theodore Bikel define chutzpah as killing your mother and father and then throwing yourself on the mercy of the court on the grounds that you're an orphan. That, as Leo Rosten maintains, is the classic definition of this great Yiddish word.[9] There are other good definitions by illustration. An excellent one from *New York Times* movie critic A. O. Scott appeared in his review of Todd Haynes's movie *I'm Not There*, based on Bob Dylan: "Robert Zimmerman, a Jewish teenager growing up in Eisenhower-era Minnesota, borrowed a name from a Welsh poet and the singing style of an Oklahoma Dust Bowl troubadour and bluffed his way into the New York folk scene," Scott writes. "That was chutzpah." This seems especially apt for a figure who is as much a self-invention as Fitzgerald's Gatsby, and who, in Scott's words, has the uncanny "ability to synthesize authenticity—to give his serial hoaxes and impersonations the ring of revealed and esoteric truth."[10]

Equally to my liking is the way the lyricist Sammy Cahn uses the term "chutzpah" in his autobiography, *I Should Care*. Sammy has been talking about the bandleader and clarinetist Artie Shaw, who made unforgettable recordings of Cole Porter's "Begin the Beguine" and "Easy to Love." Now this is what you should know about Artie Shaw: Like the rest of us, Artie had suffered as a kid from anti-Semitism even though he was born in the States and grew up here, and he was determined to be better than the goyim by gentile standards at any given activity. So, for example, he was a precision marksman, ranked fourth in the country. He was also an expert at fly-fishing. When he hired Billie Holiday it was momentous. He was the first white bandleader to hire a black female singer as a full-time member. Everyone knew Artie's recording of "Frenesi." Hell, everyone knew Artie. Short for Abraham Arthur Arshawsky, the name Artie Shaw was how some second looey learned to pronounce the French word for artichoke (*artichaut*) in 1945. Artie was brilliant, he made bundles of money, he was married eight times—what more could you want? Anyway, according to Sammy, Artie was arrogant, cocksure, and successful with women. He had "plucked" Ava Gardner, Lana Turner, and Betty Grable, and what's more, they had pursued him. He was "unobtainable," and that was part of his appeal. "If Frank Sinatra had been able to treat Ava Gardner the way Artie Shaw did, he might have held her," Cahn says.[11] When Shaw married Betty Kern, Jerome Kern's daughter, the young couple stayed for a time in the composer's home. "Artie would also tell Jerome Kern what was wrong with his songs—try and top *that* for chutzpah."[12] This sentence delights me not only because of its semantic utility but also because of what it says about the universal respect and even awe for Kern, especially after December 27, 1927, the night the curtain went up for the first time on *Show Boat* at the Ziegfeld Theater. Shaw's marriage to Betty didn't survive the war.

Speaking of Artie Shaw, Will Friedwald in his book on Sinatra credits Shaw for being possibly "the first popular musician to conceive of a standard repertory of classic American popular songs. Shaw represents the earliest exponent of a generation of musical artists who realized that there was more to pop music than this year's crop of kisses."[13] This became the Sinatra strategy on the albums he recorded for Capitol Records in the 1950s. He found his material in the treasure chests of the 1920s and 1930s and even, in the case of *On the Road to Mandalay*, in the Rudyard Kipling trunk. The best thing that could happen to an old song was to have Sinatra sing it and renew it as a modern possibility. Ruth Etting's rendition of "It All Depends on You" is wonderful, and I recommend the experience. Twenty years younger, Sinatra's version from the late 1940s demonstrates that the song is even better when done in swing time and that it retains its freshness and immediacy. One acclaimed Sinatra "concept" album, *In the Wee Small Hours of the Morning*, rescued "Ill Wind" (music Harold Arlen, lyrics Ted Koehler), "I See Your Face Before Me" (music Arthur Schwartz, lyrics Howard Dietz), and, most dramatically, "Last Night When We Were Young" (music Arlen, lyrics Yip Harburg) to the virtues of which one might have been deaf before hearing Sinatra sing it.

It was Artie Shaw who gave Melvin Howard Tormé his first big break. It was in 1946. Artie had the best saxophone section in the whole Swing Era, some of the best jazz sidemen in Hollywood, and a spectacular string section. Shaw made an album called *Artie Shaw Plays Cole Porter* and he had Mel Tormé and his vocal group, the Mel-tones, sing "What Is This Thing Called Love?" that lovely example of Porter's wizardry with blue notes, minor harmonies, and sudden changes of key from C minor to C major and back, with a full octave leap on the final keynote. Alone, Mel "warbled" (his word) "Get Out of Town," which launched his solo singing career. Mel felt that he, like Artie Shaw, owed a lot to Porter. The "soul of sophistication," Mel called him.[14]

Tormé, the son of Russian Jews, was already writing songs and playing drums in 1938 in a band led by Chico

Marx. I never saw him smile so broadly as when he sat at the drums and hit the high hat while a recording of Benny Goodman's "Sing, Sing, Sing" played behind him. With his jazz-inflected style, Tormé was one of the few vocalists from the big band era to survive and flourish as a popular singer well beyond the eclipse of the musical idiom he had mastered. He had a pure tenor voice, very boyish, and an extraordinary talent for scatting. When he became famous, he hated being called the "velvet fog," though the guy who came up with the epithet thought he was complimenting the singer's high tenor and smooth delivery. If you never caught Mel in person, you missed something. He had a great club presence. The live audience turned him on. He would have the band play the opening bars of some well-known song and prep the audience for it, and then he would fake out everybody by singing a different song to the same rhythmical arrangement. He had excellent taste. You were expecting "New York, New York" and instead you might hear "Love Is Just Around the Corner" with Leo Robin at his witty best in the release.[5] The songwriter evokes Venus de Milo, famous for her charms, and adds,

> *But strictly between us,*
> *You're cuter than Venus*

And furthermore, unlike the sculpture in the Louvre, "you" have a pair of arms.

I love that lyric. Not just the surprise, but the fact that the lyricist has figured out a witty new way to proclaim the superiority of "you" to paragons of beauty. Robin uses the A-B-B-A stanza, in which one rhyme is sandwiched between another, to perfection, with the more unusual rhyme ("Venus" and "between us") coming at you rapidly. Meanwhile, the lover's hyperbole ("Venus de Milo") is undercut by lively vernacular idioms ("cuter") as well as the reminder, which you get only in the last rhyming syllable, that the fabulous goddess of love to whom "you" are being compared is a statue, and the ruin of one at that. That's doing a lot in four lines. Leo Robin—who also wrote the words for "Diamonds Are a Girl's Best Friend" (music Jule Styne) and "Thanks for the Memory" (music Ralph Rainger)—did clever things with a lyric. Right now I'm listening to Susannah McCorkle sing "Bye Bye Baby" from *Gentlemen Prefer Blondes* (music Jule Styne). The lyric ends with the confident declaration that the singer will be seeing her "baby by and by," and so, through the agency of a pun, the valediction ("bye bye") becomes a vow.

Christmas in July

At nineteen Mel Tormé graduated from high school. There's a wonderful Preston Sturges movie called *Christmas in July* with Dick Powell, and the title has a particular application to Mel in 1945. On an exceptionally hot day that July, Mel wrote the music for "The Christmas Song," the Nat King Cole standard that begins "Chestnuts roasting on an open fire." Mel said his lyricist, Bob Wells, wrote the opening four lines in a futile effort to cool off. Nothing else—a swim in a pool, a cold shower—had done the trick, so maybe the imagination would come to the rescue. Mel saw the lines on a spiral pad and "forty-some-odd minutes later," the song came into being.[16] Those guys were always expecting a lot of their imaginations. They imagined themselves as invisibly Jewish; they made a new religion of America, and they altered it at the same time. You could argue, for instance, that Christmas became a secular holiday thanks to the efforts of Irving Berlin, who gave "White Christmas" to a fearful nation in a state of total war in 1942. That was some Christmas present. Berlin knew it, too. "I want you to take down a song I wrote over the weekend," he told his right-hand man, Helmy Kresa. "Not only is it the best song *I* ever wrote, it's the best song *anybody* ever wrote."[17]

I knew about the phenomenal sales figures of Bing Crosby's recording of the song, and how it appeared in top-forty charts for something like twenty-five straight years, and is the greatest-selling song of all time, but I grasped its full significance as a cultural artifact only when I saw Billy Wilder's *Stalag 17* (1953) with William Holden as a captive aviator in a German prisoner-of-war camp. The movie begins on a gray December day. Von Scherbach, the sadistic camp commandant played by Otto Preminger, tells the assembled men that he regrets not giving them a white Christmas "just like the ones you used to know" as "that clever little man wrote—you know, the one who stole his name from our capital—that something-or-other Berlin?" The commandant means it as a nasty crack, but to the viewer it conveys an additional message, one that might account for his bitterness. In the film's vocabulary, America has supplanted Germany, one Berlin has replaced another, and most galling of all, the upstart is an American Jew named Irving. To be sure, *Stalag 17* is full of music, and you never do hear "White Christmas." The traditional Christmas carol "Adeste Fidelis" provides the choral background for a solemn scene later in the movie, and "I Love You" (music Harry Archer, lyrics Harlan Thompson) is sung for comic and nostalgic effect. But the point about the two Berlins has been made. After all, the movie's narrator, played by Harvey Lembeck, is named Harry Shapiro. Christmas as celebrated by the GIs in Stalag 17 is a solemn but nonsectarian affair, a family tradition, with snow-white weather if you're lucky. It's a holiday that means *home*—a holiday that even guys named Shapiro get to celebrate and enjoy.

Was this altogether a blessing, this secularizing of the Christian holiday and weakening of the religious impulse? The Jews had, after all, gone down the path of total assimilation before—with disastrous results. In the first decades of the nineteenth century, the Jews won their political emancipation in Germany. According to Gershom Scholem, the struggle for civil rights was advanced as much by the French Revolution as the German Enlightenment and led to a revolutionary change: the willingness, even eagerness, with which many Jews embraced the idea that they were Germans first, Jews second. So enthusiastic were they about the transformation that they failed to note the absence of equal ardor from non-Jews—some of whom may have reasoned that a people willing to jettison its traditions may be suspect in its new loyalties. Something extraordinary and positive did ensue: "The long-buried creativity of the Jews was liberated." The Jewish passion for German culture occurred, what's more, "precisely at the moment when that culture had reached one of its most fruitful turning points. It was the zenith of Germany's bourgeois era. One can say that it was a happy hour when the newly awakened creativity of the Jews, which was to assume such impressive forms after 1780, impinged precisely on the zenith of a great creative period of the German people."[18] While some of the Jews felt they had accomplished the transition "from talmudic Judaism to the new German-Jewish way of life" in record time, this was a self-deception, and the really astonishing thing was how many people, sophisticated and open-eyed, bought the dream and began describing themselves as "being of Jewish descent." Yet they didn't want to banish entirely their Jewish identity. "It is true that very broad segments of German Jewry were ready to liquidate their peoplehood, but they also wished—in differing degrees, to be sure—to preserve their Jewishness as a kind of heritage, as a creed, as an element unknowable and indefinable, yet clearly present in their consciousness."[19] They wanted, in other words, to remain Jews in an "indefinable" sense for reasons of a sentimental attachment.

It is a painful irony that the Jews' cultural success and even intellectual "preeminence" awakened a resistance, which grew more vigorous before finally turning into virulent anti-Semitism. "To the love of the Jews for Germany there corresponded the emphatic distance with which the Germans encountered them," Scholem writes, allowing his moral outrage to find expression when he confronts "the German Jews—whose critical sense was as famous among Germans as it was irritating to them—[and who] distinguished themselves by an astounding lack of critical insight into their own situation." He is shocked at the readiness of Jews to embrace theories justifying the "sacrifice of their Jewish existence," as if the absorption into a "host" organism were the desired end for the Jew as ghostly intruder or parasitic guest. Gershom Scholem takes great pains to warn that "assimilation," whether desirable or not as a goal, was in the end a delusion. The very ambition to embrace German culture and join German society doomed the German Jews. When Jewish intellectual leaders endorsed the idea that the fulfillment of Jewish destiny was a wished-for "absorption of this people by other peoples," only the anti-Semites took such ideas to heart, seeing in them "an especially nefarious trick of the Jews, an especially conspiratorial note."[20]

Scholem writes so persuasively that anyone taking the path of assimilation—the path of least resistance—had better take note. Is it really different here, now, from there and then? Were they fooling themselves, the men and women who advocated the American secular religion and forgot about going to temple, wearing a hat, eating kosher food, and keeping the Sabbath?

You can argue that in several ways the America of the first half of the twentieth century differed from the Germany that seduced, betrayed, and ultimately tried to exterminate the Jews. American culture was always more in flux than its European counterparts. The opportunity to invent new categories of popular culture was open to American Jews with sufficient vision and capital as could never have been the case in Germany. America lacked the tradition of vicious anti-Semitism that erupted in murderous violence

in medieval and modern Europe. And the speed of technological change favored the enterprising and industrious
newcomers.

In idealizing or romanticizing America, a Jewish songwriter would inevitably change it. Irving Berlin suppressed
his own Jewish identity, but he also did something much
more dramatic and extraordinary. In a memorable riff in
Operation Shylock (1993), Philip Roth dubs Berlin "the greatest Diasporist of all" and writes, "The radio was playing
'Easter Parade' and I thought, but this is Jewish genius on a
par with the Ten Commandments. God gave Moses the Ten
Commandments and then He gave to Irving Berlin 'Easter
Parade' and 'White Christmas.' The two holidays that celebrate the divinity of Christ—the divinity that's the very
heart of the Jewish rejection of Christianity—and what
does Irving Berlin brilliantly do? He de-Christs them both!
Easter he turns into a fashion show and Christmas into a
holiday about snow." The passage is hilarious, the tone that
of a *tummler*, but the argument couldn't be more serious. "Is
that so disgraceful a means of defusing the enmity of centuries? Is anyone really dishonored by this? If schlockified
Christianity is Christianity cleansed of Jew hatred, then
three cheers for schlock. If supplanting Jesus Christ with
snow can enable my people to cozy up to Christmas, then let
it snow, let it snow, let it snow."[21] Though the passage is
unequivocal in its endorsement of Berlin's "means of defusing the enmity of centuries," note that Roth himself, whom
Jewish critics used to lecture for showing disrespect to the
fathers and the faith, could not sound more Jewish in this
passage and in *Operation Shylock* as a glorious whole.

The House I Live In

The real America did not conform exactly to the dream of the Promised Land that lured the poor shtetl-dwellers of Poland and Russia and emboldened them to endure the hardships of a treacherous journey overland to a port such as Hamburg or Antwerp followed by a transatlantic crossing in steerage among the ship's vermin and lice. But the squalid, overcrowded tenements of the Lower East Side were infinitely preferable to the constant fear and periodic eruption of homicidal violence that the immigrants left behind, and new dreams came along to take the place of the ancient rituals abandoned. The wave of pogroms and harsh new anti-Semitic laws that followed the assassination of Czar Alexander II in 1881 made life so perilous for the Jews of Russia—and the duties required of them so onerous—that leaving and braving the hazards of escape seemed the only sensible thing to do. Two million Jewish refugees (including the parents of Irving Berlin, Harold Arlen, and the Gershwins) came to the United States from Eastern Europe between 1880 and 1920. In Berlin's earliest memory he was shivering in a blanket on the side of the road watching his home burn down when he was four or five years old. It had been torched. The whole village went up in flames. The Baline family hid in a field until the Cossacks rode out of town, the danger had passed, and they were spared. It was then that the cantor Moses Baline took his wife and brood and raised enough cash to finance the land journey from Russia to Antwerp and the ocean crossing from there. So the story goes. And though certain aspects of it (Siberia, Cossacks) have been debunked as the stuff of legend or tall tale, Berlin had the chance to correct the account and chose not to do so, and the chief question is whether its truth is literal or metaphorical.

The first dream of a refugee is like that of the simple, humble soul who is summoned to heaven and is told that any wish he makes will be granted, in Isaac Leib Peretz's Yiddish tale "Bontsha the Silent." What poor unassuming Bontsha asks for is simply to have a buttered roll in the morning for breakfast. Translated into an American idiom, there is the young couple in *I'd Rather Be Right* (1937), a satirical Rodgers and Hart show about FDR: "We want so little, Mr. Roosevelt. Just the right to work, and be married to each other—and—bring up the kids. We don't want much. If we could have just that. That isn't too much to ask, is it?"[22] As a matter of fact, FDR had anticipated the question and answered it affirmatively in his second inaugural address on January 20 of that year. He saw "one-third of a nation illhoused, ill-clad, ill-nourished." And in a speech given in January of 1941, he forecast a world founded on "four freedoms," including not only the First Amendment rights to speak and to worship as one pleases but the frankly utopian "freedom from want" and "freedom from fear." The Great Depression notwithstanding, the immigrants had their dream and lived it. They found work, married each other, and had kids, and the kids became American as fast as they could, spoke

English, disdained Yiddish, chewed gum, drank Coke, played stickball, created *Superman* comics and *Mad* magazine, disliked Hebrew School, and didn't want to know from Europe, the old world, the past.

To the children of the refugees, America remained a realm of possibility. The pursuit of happiness was a genial right guaranteed less by decree than by a condition of upward social mobility unknown in the old country. In America you could climb the stairway to paradise penalty-free. You could start from scratch on a blank slate. That was the illusion, anyway. Of all the gifts America offered, this was the one that you could end up regretting most bitterly. Yet the foreknowledge didn't stop you from greedily embracing the seductive illusion that the past could be banished, made to disappear, to give up its hold on us.

Gershwin family legend has it that on the voyage from Hamburg to New York, the paterfamilias—Moses, or Moishe, Gershowitz of St. Petersburg, Russia—lost the note bearing the address of his one relative in the United States. He had written the name and address on a piece of paper and tucked it under his hat, but the wind blew his hat into the sea.[23] Apocryphal or not, the story is a nice metaphor for the plight of the newcomer greeted by the "Mother of Exiles" in New York harbor. Coming to America was a heady gamble: You had to throw more than caution to the winds; your identity was as thin as a piece of paper, and so Moishe became Morris and Gershowitz became Gershvin first and then Gershwin. But the sons—George (born Jacob, or Yakov) especially but also Ira (Isidore, or Izzy)—not only got to live the American dream but could proffer their own romantic version of it. "Strike Up the Band," "Fascinating Rhythm," "Nice Work If You Can Get It," "I've Got a Crush on You," "Embraceable You," " 'S Wonderful," "Love Is Here to Stay."

If success in America is most easily measured in material terms, you—hero or heroine of the American dream—undertake a pilgrim's progress between failure and success. Like the rook in chess, you can go up or down or sideways and more than one space at a time. The goal is to reach the top, and the old religion is a hindrance. It is, at the least, maximally inconvenient to keep kosher and observe the Sabbath if you worship the gods of status and success. There was always more than one reason to keep a low Jewish profile. To play down your religious affiliation follows directly from the suspicion that anti-Semitism persists; and just to remind you that you're not being paranoid (which is justifiable anyway since, as Delmore Schwartz observed, even paranoids have enemies), every so often a drunken actor or angry community leader delivers a tirade blaming the world's ills on the Jews.

What takes the place of religion when you banish it? America itself was the American dreamer's answer to the question. America is a religion as well as a romance—it is indeed the religion you practice when, for example, you celebrate the freedom of religion you enjoy in America. Take "The House I Live In," the song Frank Sinatra sings in the celebrated ten-minute short of the same name in 1945. Preaching religious tolerance, the song became a big hit, and Hollywood congratulated itself righteously on the movie. It didn't fit in any of the conventional categories, so the Academy awarded it an honorary Oscar.[24] In the film, the Sinatra character intercedes to stop a crowd of kids from bullying a boy who looks like the rest but is from a "different" religion. The song that civilizes the crowd and makes good citizens out of bigots begins with the twice-asked question: "What is America to me?" According to Abel Meeropol's idealistic lyrics, the answer starts with the Bill of Rights, but the dominant image is that of a house where everyone belongs, all are equal, and the people feel free. America houses all colors and creeds, though none in particular is specified.[25] The words "Jew" and "Christian" are never uttered in the song. It's as though religious differentiation and disputation were beside the point given this new dream we have to worship. American democracy—as an idea, a potential rather than actual condition—has come along to fill the void that the philosophers created when they declared that God had died.

"The House I Live In" ends with a musical echo of the end of "America the Beautiful": "from sea to shining sea." The voice is the magical voice of the young Sinatra, and so are the sentiments—the Sinatra of 1945 was an exemplary liberal. But the words, the tune, and the script came from three left-wing gentlemen who were trying to reconcile the rival gods of America and of socialism. Albert Maltz wrote the screenplay, Earl Robinson wrote the song's music, and Abel Meeropol supplied the lyrics. Unfortunately, the subsequent lives of the three men expose the democratic idealism of the song—a proud assertion of the right of free speech—as a species of wishful thinking. Maltz refused to name names for the House Un-American Activities Committee (HUAC) in 1947, was cited for Contempt of Congress, became one of the Hollywood Ten, and served his time. Robinson would also be blacklisted in the McCarthy era. Meeropol, who wrote under the pen name Lewis Allan, had written the words of "Strange Fruit," the anti-lynching song that Billie Holiday sang. With his wife, Meeropol would later adopt the orphan sons of the executed spies Julius and Ethel Rosenberg. I have listened to "The House I Live In" a dozen times asking myself what makes it "left-wing," subversive, or suspect. There are three possible phrases that HUAC could have taken exception to: the "worker by my side," the "right to speak my mind out," and "especially the people."

Religion may have been, as Karl Marx termed it, "the opium of the masses," an ideology with which to con, manipulate, or drug the mob, but that did not lessen the need for a substitute, a religion that might somehow be made consistent with the post-Darwinian skepticism of the secular state. You could, as some did, choose to make politics your religion. Bad choice: That way disappointment lies. Politics in the world of the immigrants usually meant Socialism ("in my childhood the only Jewish religion that could take [my father] out of himself," said Alfred Kazin) or Marxism, the god that failed.[26] Another alternative was art. Like an action painter, you could serve the muse and elevate art into a god and aesthetics into a theology. Or you could turn to mass culture as the place to establish a new secular religion, a religion in modern dress. Not everyone thought this last was a noble endeavor. Alfred Kazin, in his memoir *New York Jew*, recalls that to the Upper West Side intellectuals of the postwar years, " 'Mass culture' was the opium of the boobs. It explained the failure of Socialism in America. It was sometimes called 'popular culture' and could make a sociologist out of any literary intellectual."[27]

During the war, the need to combat Hitler's ideological fanaticism was constant, and on the creators and purveyors of American popular culture fell the burden. Like a perverted brand of religious dogma, Nazi doctrine consisted of articles of faith blindly affirmed despite the contradictory evidence of one's eyes, mind, books, memory, and history. Nazism was a religion "complete with Messiah, a holy book, a cross, the trappings of religious pageantry, a priesthood of black-robed and anointed elite, excommunication and death for heretics, and the millennial promise of the Thousand Year Reich."[28] Not by military means alone could the Nazis be defeated. What was needed was a religious force of belief and conviction that could effectively oppose the swastika in the white circle against a red field. But how could you do it? If "White Christmas" secularized a religious holiday, could you do the opposite and lift the secular world of popular song into the realm of the religious hymn?

God Bless America

The nights of November 9 and 10, 1938, marked the point of no return in Hitler's plot to murder the Jewish people. On those nights in Germany and Austria the Nazis perpetrated pogroms more vicious and of wider magnitude than any before. It was then that the Nazis demonstrated their mastery of the mob, their control of media and message, and their intent to make a program of persecution the prelude to a campaign of extermination. The ostensible cause of the attacks on the Jews was the assassination of a minor official in the German embassy in Paris. Herschel Grynszpan, a distraught seventeen-year-old Jewish boy from Germany, pulled the trigger, he said, "in the name of twelve thousand persecuted Jews."[29] Just a few days before, word had reached Grynszpan that his parents and sister were among the Polish-born Jews whom the Germans had deported and deposited in a Polish border town called Zbasyn.

Grynszpan had unwittingly provided the Nazis with a pretext and, in the person of the minor embassy official, a martyr. The ninth of November was, in Hitler's mind, not only the day in 1918 when Germany was stabbed in the back, the day Kaiser Wilhelm was made to abdicate and the country officially lost World War I. It was all that, yes, but it had also become a sacred day in the Nazi calendar—the day of Hitler's failed Beer-Hall Putsch in Munich in 1923. When news of the Paris shooting reached propaganda minister Goebbels's ears, he issued a directive demanding inflammatory front-page coverage of the assassination. At the same time, the Nazis shut down all Jewish publications and banned Jewish children from German schools. With stage-managed spontaneity, the Nazi-inflamed mob enthusiastically set synagogues on fire, beat and humiliated Jews, destroyed their property, and took their homes away as uniformed police looked on. The shop windows of Jewish stores were smashed, and it was the sound of those windows shattering that gave the date its infamous name: Kristallnacht. Seventy-five hundred stores were destroyed. One hundred ninety-one synagogues went up in smoke. In some cases, the Jewish victims were charged with arson; in others they were arrested—allegedly for their own protection. Thirty thousand were sent to concentration camps.

Sanctioned by Nazi Party leaders and carried out with fanatical zeal, Kristallnacht seems in retrospect to have served Hitler as a kind of trial run for his more ambitious genocidal enterprises. The Nazi brass knew that in Evian-les-Bains (France) the previous summer, an international conference on the Jewish refugee problem had left it unsolved. The lack of a meaningful response to Kristallnacht confirmed Hitler's conviction that England and France would not a risk a military showdown over the fate of the Jewish people. He had previously banked on the belief that Czechoslovakia and the Rhineland were not of such great consequence to the Western powers. They would huff and puff over the regrettable development, and that would be it. In all those instances he gambled and won. On September 1, 1939, he would bet the same on Poland, which was one wager too many. But in the case of the Jewish refugees, Hitler guessed right. Nobody wanted them. He felt he had a free hand to deport as many as he could round up, to make them disappear in night and fog.

Nothing of comparable import happened in the United States on November 11, 1938. Newspapers expressed outrage over the events in Germany and Austria. The journalist Dorothy Thompson took up the case and made the public aware of Nazi injustices. But something did happen in America that in its own way took note of the twentieth anniversary of the end of World War I. Now called Veterans'

Day, it was then still called Armistice Day, and the singer Kate Smith needed a new song for her radio show. Irving Berlin took an old song out of his trunk and refashioned it into "God Bless America," and on November 11, 1938, Kate Smith sang it for the first time on the radio. She sang it again on her Thanksgiving show and then weekly thereafter. The song became immensely popular. They played it at Ebbets Field in Brooklyn on Memorial Day 1940, and the Dodger fans rose and took off their hats as for the national anthem.[30] It was played at the Republican National Convention that nominated Wendell Willkie and again when the Democrats got together to nominate FDR for an unprecedented third term. A movement arose to replace the "Star-Spangled Banner"—always a challenge for a singer—with Berlin's new song. (The composer would hear none of it. "There's only one national anthem, which can never be replaced.")

Long established as the patriotic song of choice in the United States, "God Bless America" returned to airwaves and stadium public address systems in a big way after September 11, 2001. After the events of that day, when the catastrophe was fresh and a crisis atmosphere prevailed, it was obligatory to hear it sung in reverent silence or to join in the singing during the seventh-inning stretch of baseball games.[31] Mind you, "God Bless America" was not always so universally beloved. Protests were incited by the anti-Semites of the late 1930s, the clerics and columnists that Philip Roth brings to frightening life in his novel *The Plot Against America*, a nightmare version of history in which Charles Lindbergh defeats Franklin Roosevelt for the presidency. Some critics taxed "God Bless America" for being "flag-waving, sentimental, jingoistic"; the left never liked the song, preferring Woody Guthrie's "This Land Is Your Land." What vociferous others held against it was that it was the creation of a refugee, "Izzy Balinsky, ex–Singing Waiter," and the commercial product of Tin Pan Alley. A parody lyric beginning "God lives in Hollywood—he just planed in" made the rounds. In some quarters, the song was despised above all because its author was a Jew.[32] Ingenious arguments were employed against Berlin. The manager of a radio station wrote an open letter demanding that the songwriter turn over to the public all royalties from "God Bless America," because "you, Mr. Berlin, have no more right to a personal interest in 'God Bless America' than the descendants of Abraham Lincoln have a right to a restricting copyright on the Gettysburg Address. That great document passed into the public domain as the words fell from his lips," and the same should happen with Berlin's song. Berlin, supported by ASCAP, stuck to his guns and prevailed.[33] A true believer, he then turned around and donated the proceeds of the song—among the best-selling songs of all time—to the Boy Scouts and Girl Scouts of America.

It is not my intention to say that Berlin intended his song to be a response to or a comment on what was happening in Germany. Nothing of the kind. But it was not a mere coincidence that Irving Berlin's song was first heard in American households on the same day that many read about Nazi atrocities visited on Jewish households and shops. "God Bless America" became as popular as it did because of its virtues as a song and because it was what the country desperately needed. It is as much a religious hymn as it is a patriotic anthem, and in the terms of Newtonian mechanics it represented an equal and opposite force pressing back against the Nazis' martial cadenzas. The same idea animates a famous scene in *Casablanca* (1942), another great cultural artifact that was largely the product of Jewish writers working for a Jewish studio head in Hollywood during the war. The Germans in uniform are singing a chauvinistic German march in Rick's Café. Resistance fighter Paul Henreid finds this intolerable and leads the rest of the cast in an impromptu rendition of the "Marseillaise," which finally drowns out the German song—just as the "Marseillaise" itself at the end of Tchaikovsky's *1812 Overture* is defeated by the principal theme of the Russian national anthem.

Irving Berlin militated in favor of America during World War II. When he donned an army uniform and sang to entertain the troops, the newsreel footage may have done as much to combat anti-Semitism as Hank Greenberg's fifty-eight homers for Detroit a few seasons earlier. America was surely the religion Berlin preached. Berlin's daughter Mary recalls her "double heritage" as unreservedly good. It gives her pleasure to think "of the Berlin Christmas, with its prelude the Berlin Hanukkah, and of the way my parents, the former Miss Mackay and the eminently Jewish Mr. Berlin, managed to fashion out of their differences a set of traditions and rituals that remain among my fondest childhood pleasures."[34]

And yet—and yet—Mary Ellin Barrett also recalls grasping, around the age of nine, "why we did not buy toys marked 'Made in Germany,' to half-grasp the meaning of my father's Russian village going up in flames, of the word 'pogrom,' " and later she became aware of "the crazies who asked what right an immigrant Jew had to call on God to bless America."[35] Yes, you can talk all you want about assimilation and the secular impulse and the bitch goddess success and the American dream. In the end, the Jew is still a Jew. The joke about two men, a banker and a hunchback, who meet in the street, comes to mind. Both men were born Jewish, but the banker has joined a wealthy Episcopalian church. He says: "Did you know that I was once Jewish?" "Yes," says the other, "and I was once a hunchback." The psychoanalyst Theodor Reik, who tells this joke, concludes that "it is as difficult for the Jew to get rid of his Jewishness as it is for the ancient mariner to lose the albatross."[36] More difficult, actually (I would say), for the mariner in Coleridge's poem is able to shake off the albatross from the moment he blesses the slimy creatures of the great deep— before half the poem is over—whereas for the Jews it's the same as for the Jets in the opening number in *West Side Story:* When you're a Jew, you're a Jew all the way.

VII

A Right to Sing the Blues

What did I do to be so black and blue?
ANDY RAZAF, "Black and Blue"

Yankee Doodle *Yiddishkeit*

Much of twentieth-century pop culture is a kind of Yankee Doodle *Yiddishkeit*," Jody Rosen writes in his book *White Christmas*.[1] The association of Jews and show business is casually but universally acknowledged. Yet even the incontrovertible fact that many American songwriters were Jewish is not unambiguous. Some were more Jewish than others, and this is so whether you use lineage, upbringing, assertion, or behavior as your criterion. Back in 1965 Robert Alter noted that most of "the so-called American Jewish writers" were "culturally American in all important respects and only peripherally or vestigially Jewish."[2] The same was true of Jerome Kern, Irving Berlin, and company. From the first, Richard Rodgers, for example, took the theater far more seriously than the temple. In his autobiography he identifies himself as Jewish "for socioethnic reasons rather than because of any deep religious conviction."[3] What are "socioethnic reasons"? According to David Ewen's 1957 biography of Rodgers, he occasionally attended services at Temple Emanu-el in New York, partly to please his wife and partly out of a "sentimental attachment to his racial background." Rodgers felt a "social rather than religious" connection to other Jews. "Besides he believes strongly that 'when anybody who is a member of a minority can accomplish something important, he should declare himself so that this minority can become a little less minor.' "[4]

This is eloquent, but it leaves the question largely unanswered. What does it mean to be Jewish for "socioethnic reasons" or out of a "sentimental attachment to [one's] racial background"? The sentences imply that Rodgers has made a deliberate choice: "he believes strongly." But what does this belief amount to? That the speaker, while not affirming his religious identity, doesn't deny it either? Well, yes and no: Ambivalence is a dominant note. Thus, a Gershwin biographer writes that Gershwin "was never the young Jew in Manhattan struggling to break free of the ghetto. He was not ashamed of his roots, but he did not glorify them. There is no doubt, however, that he was ambitious and sought recognition, but not because he was determined to overcome his Jewishness."[5] All those negatives in successive clauses—*never, not, not, no, not*—compromise the assertions and inject the doubt that "no doubt" was meant to exclude. Does the idea that Judaism can persist as a "socioethnic" category or a "sentimental attachment" mask the defensive recognition that you're a Jew if you're a Jew in the eyes of the *goyim*—that it's a birthright, impossible to shed, no matter how earnest the effort? Thus the same Gershwin biographer quotes the English writer Osbert Sitwell's remark that Gershwin "possessed a fine racial appearance; nobody could mistake him for anyone but a Jew."[6]

Jean-Paul Sartre made what you might call the default argument—that Jewish identity arises from global anti-Semitism—which Patricia Erens, in her fine book on the Jew in American movies, is right to characterize as a weak defense.[7] It has been said that Eastern Europe in the past several decades has proved that you can have anti-Semitism without Jews. But could you, can you, have Jews without Judaism? As acculturation turns into assimilation, do the Jews retain their Jewishness only in some attenuated way as a demographic tag, a voting bloc, a special-interest group, or a sociological construct? Instead of the *tallis* and *tefillin*, the lighting of the candles on Friday night and the *havdallah* ceremony when the Sabbath ends, the public opinion pollsters give you a demographic profile, more than a stereotype but less than an individual: a college-educated professional who probably still votes Democratic, supports the state of Israel, values humor and the life of the mind, has a special affection for *Fiddler on the Roof*, and *kvells* every time a play-by-play man says that the greatest pitcher of all time is Sandy Koufax, a Jew who didn't pitch on the high holy days of October 1965 even though his team was playing in the World Series.

The American dream, define it as you may, is a secular deal. "The children of immigrants sought to Americanize themselves as quickly as possible, and they were careful not to betray their ethnic origins or heritage," Irving Howe writes in *World of Our Fathers*. "In the twenties and thirties they divorced themselves almost completely from formal religion, and it seemed as though Judaism could no longer sustain itself in America." The kids of greenhorns couldn't wait to become American. They wanted to speak American English, not Yiddish or German, and without that accursed Central or Eastern European accent. Immigration promised survival to one generation, and assimilation promised the romance of life, liberty, and the pursuit of happiness to the next. Your name can be Irving and you can go to City College and become an important literary intellectual and recall with shame how you cringed when, as a boy playing in the streets of the Bronx, you heard your father call you: "Oivie! Oivie!" Why be Marjorie Morgenstern, daughter of Rose and Arnold Morgenstern, middle-class Jews who live on Central Park West, when you can lead an ever so much more romantic life as Marjorie Morningstar (played by Natalie Wood) sharing digs in Greenwich Village with a caddish composer (played by Gene Kelly)?[8]

And still the notion persists that the assimilated Jew can remain proudly Jewish in a "socioethnic" or cultural sense— which I think implies something substantive beyond the nostalgia to which people insecure about the future are prone. The Jewishness of American songwriters inheres in their mannerisms, their choice of words, their sense of self, and it enters their songs. What I have in mind is something deeper though less direct than the moral seriousness that characterizes Oscar Hammerstein's pleas for tolerance or Yip Harburg's Depression-era ballad of the common man, "Brother, Can You Spare a Dime?"[9] Gershwin, who enjoyed all the perquisites of secular success, is said to have spoken Yiddish with Edward G. Robinson (born Emmanuel Goldenberg in Bucharest) and to have referred to himself as "this little Jewish boy," who didn't like walking in Kay Swift's Yorkville neighborhood, heavily populated as it was by German Americans, some of them noisily pro-Nazi.[10] The persistence of Yiddish, even if only sporadic, says something. When Harold Arlen, composer of *The Wizard of Oz*, wrote a birthday poem for the seventy-seven-year-old Irving Berlin, composer of "Easter Parade" and "White Christmas," Arlen incorporated the Yiddish phrase *Svet gornisht helfin* ("It's no use") and signed with his Hebrew name. Deep down, it was still Chaim Arluck communicating with Israel Baline, one cantor's son schmoozing with another, two Yeshiva *buchers* on a secular holiday in Hollywood or New York. Arlen was in some ways the most Jewish of the composers, though this had nothing to do with Jewish custom and law. His lyricists described the superstitious rituals he would follow before sitting down at the piano to write. Harold "lowered his eyes, brought his hands together, and put himself in a worshipful state of mind."[11] He had "an almost supernatural belief in 'inspiration.' He never would approach the simplest musical requirement or idea without first calling upon 'the fellow up there'—jabbing his finger at the ceiling."[12] What else is this but the religious impulse redirected toward an aesthetic end? "Get Happy," "Ill Wind," "My Shining Hour," and the rest were gifts bestowed by a deity responsive to Arlen's prayers.

To Be So Black and Blue

The dynamics of cultural exchange between Jews and African Americans is a subject so conducive to controversy and misunderstanding that many a jazz enthusiast would walk miles to avoid it. While that is my own impulse as well, the subject is closer to the center than to the periphery of any discussion of popular song in general and its specifically Jewish character. A few things are beyond dispute. Both groups have suffered injustice, persecution, prejudice, oppression; both were more or less eager to take part in the American adventure but suspicious of it, too. The two groups formed a natural political alliance under the umbrella of the Democratic coalition that prevailed for all but eight years in the period between 1933, when FDR took office, and 1969, when Richard Nixon succeeded LBJ. Finally, both groups could appeal to the story of Exodus—and the deferred dream of the Promised Land—as a redemptive narrative of their own experience. Each could imagine seeing the other in the mirror.

A distinctive trait of the popular songs written by Jewish songwriters is their "black-and-blue" edge, their foretaste of loss in the midst of joy. For example, the mixing up of anticipatory pleasure and loss animates an Irving Berlin simile in "Cheek to Cheek": It's a curious compliment that you pay a girl when you tell her that she makes your worries "vanish like a gambler's lucky streak." What kind of luck is she bringing you? You may argue that the cantor wailing in the morning prayers has his musical affinity with the saxophonist in the smoky cellar—and what's more, that the saxophonist may be playing a song written by the cantor's son. In *Stomping the Blues* (1976), Albert Murray writes that "African Americans often play the blues to get rid of the blues. Jews wail to relieve their melancholy," and the double meaning of "blues" (a melancholy mood or a song designed to express and expel it) makes the broad analogy particularly useful.[13] There is a fatalistic undertow in the blues as a verse form. Take Bessie Smith's "Empty Bed Blues." As in most blues songs, the first line of every three-line stanza is repeated, as if to underline the inevitability of the story and its potentially universal application. It's a sad story, in the end, because the heroine loses her "good lovin' " to a double-crossing friend, but along the way she gets to express the heat of sexual passion, and the song serves up humor with its woe: He brought her "first cabbage" to the boil, and he "made it awful hot." (When he inserts "the bacon," her pot runneth over.) In the American songs of Jewish song writers, something similar happens. Wit and humor give the human heart some protective dignity even when it is most exposed. It's anybody's story, and it doesn't so much unfold as recur. That long, long road gets lonelier and tougher. But with a song in my heart I'll get by. Notice the emphatic "again" in Lorenz Hart's "I Wish I Were in Love Again" and also in the line "Thank god I can be oversexed again," where "oversexed" rhymes with "vexed" and "perplexed," in "Bewitched, Bothered, and Bewildered."

That the classic American songbook owes much to the inventions, the vitality, and the heritage of African

American music is also beyond dispute. The contributions of black lyricists such as Andy Razaf ("What Did I Do to Be So Black and Blue?") and Henry Creamer ("After You've Gone") are considerable. Fats Waller ("Ain't Misbehavin' ") is a major figure as a songwriter and performer. Scott Joplin's rags, W. C. Handy's "St. Louis Blues" (1914), Duke Ellington's songs ("Mood Indigo," "Satin Doll," "It Don't Mean a Thing If It Ain't Got That Swing") and other compositions, the arrangements of Count Basie, the riffs and licks of Louis Armstrong, and other events of such magnitude in the history of jazz had an enormous influence on the "Jewish tunes" of Tin Pan Alley and Broadway.

The musical alliance of Jews and blacks held benefits for both groups. When Benny Goodman, the King of Swing, hired the black Teddy Wilson to be the pianist in his trio in 1935, it was momentous. Popular music had preceded even Major League baseball in promoting racial integration and acceptance. The Jewish songwriters created great material for African American jazz singers and musicians to perform, and we are the richer for their collaboration. In my living room I would illustrate the point by playing John Coltrane's elaborations of "My Favorite Things" on his tenor sax followed by the Nat Cole Trio's performance of "Embraceable You." I'd play Joe Williams singing "Alone Together" (music Arthur Schwartz, lyrics Howard Dietz) and Johnny Hartman, "You Are Too Beautiful" (Rodgers and Hart), and I'd ask you which you prefer. I have an admirable CD devoted to "All of Me" (music Gerald Marks, lyrics Seymour Simons), which includes versions of that evergreen by Dinah Washington, Billie Holiday, Duke Ellington (with an elegant Johnny

Hodges solo on alto sax), Count Basie, Frank Sinatra, and others. But first, here's Art Tatum playing "You Took Advantage of Me" (music Richard Rodgers, lyrics Lorenz Hart) on the piano as if that one instrument constituted an orchestra.

In *Hip: The History* John Leland writes that the "collisions" of blacks and Jews, "when black migrants from the South poured into the same cities as Jewish immigrants from eastern Europe, defined the American city as a hip hive of ethnicity and back talk."[14] The choice of "collisions" in that sentence is shrewd, for it is sometimes assumed that the interests of Jews and African Americans, in the cultural as well as the political sphere, necessarily clashed at least some of the time. Some commentators contend that Jewish songwriters helped themselves to African American musical idioms in acts of thievery that you can characterize as dastardly, ingenious, or both. In 1931, Howard Cowell, the composer who was Gershwin's music teacher, defined jazz as "Negro minstrel music as interpreted by Tin-Pan-Alley New Yorkers of Hebrew origin."[15] Jazz, according to Gershwin's early biographer Isaac Goldberg, "reaches from the black South to the black North, but in between it has been touched by the commercial wand of the Jew."[16] The allegation that the Jews had "stolen jazz" goes back to the preface Samson Raphaelson wrote in 1925 for the stage version of *The Jazz Singer*, which preceded the Warner Brothers film.[17] Raphaelson declared that Jews such as Irving Berlin, George Gershwin, Al Jolson, and Sophie Tucker "are determining the nature and scope of jazz more than any other race— more than the Negroes, from whom they have stolen jazz and given it a new color and meaning."

The idea that Jews appropriated what was properly African American has found new academic advocates. Michael Rogin and Jeffrey Melnick are among those who have advanced the idea that Gershwin in *Porgy and Bess* exemplified "the Jewish white negro." The scholars employ complicated arguments to make the case that the Jewish portrayal of self as black was meant to elevate the Jew's own status as a white ethnic.[18] It is said specifically of the minstrelsy in *The Jazz Singer*—in which Al Jolson blackens his face and sings songs glorifying Mammy and Dixie—that it was a sort of alchemical device to turn the Jew from a despised refugee into just another white ethnic in the melting pot of American life. Jolson's character in *The Jazz Singer*, Jack Robin, "plays a person of color instead of being confused for one. By painting himself black he washes himself white," Michael Rogin writes in *Blackface, White Noise*. To which Michael Alexander replies, "there are more straightforward ways for someone to demonstrate he is white than by acting black."[19]

You can paraphrase the debate about jazz, race, and religion crudely in a pair of rhetorical questions. Did the Jews or the African Americans get there first, where "there" refers to the holy land of jazz and swing? Who ripped off whom? Isaac Goldberg noted the kinship between the "Negro blue note" and the "blue note" of Hasidic chant. If you put Yiddish and black together, Goldberg added, "they spell Al Jolson." Jolson is a central figure in the debate. There are those who regard the use of blackface in any context as an insult to black people, and Jolson blackened his face in *The Jazz Singer*. End of discussion. But if you want to keep the conversation going, you might consider that black-face existed as "ethnic mimicry," in Irving Howe's phrase, until Jewish performers adopted the conventions of the genre "and transformed it into something emotionally richer and more humane."[20] And you will regard Jolson's blackface scene in *The Jazz Singer*—when he is backstage, preparing for his moment in the lights—not as prejudicial but as rich in metaphoric implication, a subtle exploration of the singer's identity as a Jew and as an American. The importance of the scene in fact is not that it exemplifies minstrelsy but that it defines the American identity dilemma, for when he is in blackface, Jolson is caught between selves—his native self and the self that has reinvented itself as American. Jolson's confrontation with his image in the mirror is an iconic moment for reasons that have less to do with race than with the fluidity of identity in secular America.

Show Boat and *Porgy and Bess*

Together with *The Jazz Singer* (1927) and Gershwin's *Porgy and Bess* (1935), *Show Boat* is one of three crucial instances of the Jewish imagination cloaking itself behind a black mask and borrowing musical idioms from jazz and the blues. It is not merely incidental that a couple of New Yorkers who had never laid eyes on the Mississippi River wrote "Ol' Man River" to be sung by a chorus of African Americans to dramatize their plight and universalize it to state the human condition. The music rises an octave and a sixth, and Hammerstein's lyric contrasts the fear and fatigue of mere mortals with the flow of the mighty Mississippi, the surging and irresistible force of life itself. The song has taken on the status of a spiritual or folk song in the truest sense. Winston Churchill alluded to it in a rousing speech he gave to the House of Commons in the summer of 1940 and then sang the song with gusto in the car going back to 10 Downing Street.

For "Can't Help Lovin' Dat Man," Kern also borrowed from spirituals and the blues. According to the libretto, the song is one that a white woman wouldn't know. Julie, who sings "Can't Help Lovin' Dat Man" and "Bill," is expelled from the riverboat troupe when she is exposed as a light-skinned black passing as white. It is impossible to watch *Show Boat* without feeling sympathetic to Julie and hostile to her racist accusers, so in the simplest and most direct sense the work opposes prejudice. But complicated things are going on here. It's as if, as Kurt List liked to say, the Jew has depicted the black man as the American version of himself. In List's allegorical reading, Julie is like the Jewish girl who falls for the gentile in tales of the *shtetl*, and *Show Boat* itself can be reduced to

a few short tales about Kern's ancestral country, in which America may be said to play the role of the *staedtel* [*sic*], with its *goyim*—some good, some bad—and its Jews, here Negroes. A favorite theme of Western ghetto tales—the story of the Jewish girl falling in love with the Gentile—is here employed twice, though in American terms: once as the marriage of the Negro girl Julie to a white man, with the attendant disapproval of the white community, and once as the well-born Magnolia's marriage to Ravenal, the good-for-nothing gambler, under the disapproval of her family. As in all moral Western ghetto stories, the protagonists draw their strength from a song of comfort. In the ghetto tales, it is always "Kol Nidre"; in *Show Boat* it is "Ol' Man River."[21]

Show Boat was the nearest thing to a genuine American folk opera until *Porgy and Bess* came along eight years later. Without Julie in *Show Boat* you would not have had Bess eight years later. And *Porgy and Bess* may be the most enduring of all of George Gershwin's ambitious efforts to wed the conventions of popular song with the structures and idioms of "serious" music. Leonard Bernstein maintained that with *Porgy and Bess* "the real destiny of Gershwin begins to be clear. . . . With *Porgy* you suddenly realize that Gershwin was a great, great theater composer."[22] The titles of the songs themselves tell the operatic tale. Summertime, and the living is easy. It ain't necessarily so. A woman is a sometime thing. A redheaded woman makes a choo-choo jump the tracks. Bess, you is my woman now. I loves you, Porgy. There's a boat that's leaving soon for New York. Where's my Bess? I'm on my way to a heavenly land.

Gershwin insisted on using black performers exclusively, and over the years productions of *Porgy and Bess* have featured such talents as Todd Duncan and Anne Brown, Leontyne Price, William Warfield, Cab Calloway, Brock Peters, Sidney Poitier, Dorothy Dandridge, Diahann Carroll, Sammy Davis, Jr., and Pearl Bailey. The libretto's representation of African Americans—poor uneducated folk who fight, drink, pimp, and get high—has offended more than a few. When the New York City Opera revived *Porgy and Bess* in the 1960s, Harold Schonberg of *The New York Times* pronounced it "not a good opera. It is not a good anything . . . and in light of recent developments, it is embarrassing. 'Porgy and Bess' contains as many stereotypes in its way as 'Uncle Tom's Cabin.' "[3] To such objections, one might reply that the "embarrassment" is extrinsic to the drama—it is what the critic has brought to the table. *Porgy and Bess* may echo the racial stereotypes of its time, but it goes beyond them. The characters are superior to their assigned roles because they express themselves in magnificent music and because both their conflicts and their aspirations are universal. The hero, the goat-cart beggar, is a crippled black man, deprived of the use of his legs but with hands powerful enough to kill his rival, the ever-dangerous Crown, in a fistfight—and this is all happening on stage at the very instant when "that man in the White House," the redoubtable president of the United States, is a crippled white man able to move only in a wheelchair—a technological improvement on the goat-cart, to be sure, but one that operates on the same basic principle.

As to the "appropriation" argument, Virgil Thomson had already articulated it in 1935: "Folk-lore subjects recounted by an outsider are only valid as long as the folk in question is unable to speak for itself, which is certainly not true of the American Negro in 1935." But this argument, if logically extended and indiscriminately applied, would punish writers adopting the point of view of any class or group to which they do not belong. We would feel the obligation to dismiss male point-of-view novels written by women, or the opposite, let alone books by pseudonymous authors of unidentified sex, class, religion, and race.

The fallacy of historical superiority would have us resist the impulse to judge the past by the standards of the present day. And where does legitimate influence end and appropriation begin? The question is both rhetorical (in that it has no specific answer) and academic (in that it may be discussed eternally without resolution or consequence). I persist in agreeing with Cynthia Ozick that the musical linkage between Jews and blacks reflects a state of "conscious mutual sympathy." It was perhaps inevitable that members of either group would lean on the other or borrow elements of its mythology or lore. Gershwin immersed himself in the musical idioms he heard in black nightclubs and churches. By the same token, let us not disregard the profound effect of the Hebrew Bible on African Americans. In "Black and Blue," Andy Razaf's lyric identifies the ebony color of the singer's skin with the biblical "mark of Ham," Noah's disrespectful son. But a far more famous example of African American borrowing from the Hebrew Bible presents itself in the spiritual "Go Down, Moses."

> *Go down, Moses,*
> *Way down in Egypt's land;*
> *Tell old Pharaoh*
> *Let my people go!*

The bondage of the Jews in Egypt, their liberation, their sojourn in the wilderness, and their pursuit of the holy land have served generations of African Americans as an allegory and a model, and they continue to do so today. In a November 2008 *New Yorker* article, David Remnick quotes a speech President-elect Barack Obama gave in 2007 to "older" civil-rights leaders and black children. Obama addressed "the Joshua generation," his generation, which had succeeded "the Moses generation," whose leaders "didn't cross over the river to see the Promised Land," just as Moses himself, in Deuteronomy, is vouchsafed a view of the land of milk and honey but never sets foot in it.

The matter is not easily dismissed. Such are the complexities of racial and religious identity that Obama himself, when running for a congressional seat in Chicago in the late 1990s, was assailed by a rival as "the white man in blackface in our community." [24] It's as if the fact of being black is not enough to establish the authenticity of one's claim to be black—as if "black" were a metaphor or a piece of discourse rather than an objective reality. The ready illustration that comes to hand is the psychological warfare Muhammad Ali used on George Foreman before their heavyweight championship fight in Zaire in 1974. Ali and his handlers insinuated that Foreman, whose skin color was darker than Ali's, was not the black man in this fight. The terms of discourse are colored with prejudice, even when the prejudice is inverted to reflect an inversion in the black-white paradigm. The terms remain as charged as the political relations between groups of erstwhile allies whose interests have diverged and clashed. But the larger point that Ali made in his taunts and dismissals of Foreman was that the African American community has its own version of identity doubt.

The Jazz Singer

Sholom Aleichem wrote a Passover story called "On Account of a Hat." In it, Sholem Shachnah is explaining what has delayed his return to Kasrilevke from a business trip. It seems he has fallen asleep at the platform waiting for his train, is wakened by the porter as the train comes in, and in his rush to board the train, grabs not his own hat but that of the Russian official sitting beside him on the bench—a military hat with a red band and a visor. On the train everyone treats Sholem Shachnah with great respect. He is whisked into a first-class compartment. People salute him and call him "Your excellency." But when in the corridor he chances to see himself in a mirror, he "sees not himself but the official with the red band. That's who it is!" He curses the porter. "Twenty times I tell him to wake me and I even give him a tip, and what does he do, that dumb ox, may he catch cholera in his face, but wake the official instead! And me he leaves asleep on the bench!" So Sholem Shachnah races back to the station in order to wake himself up. But no sooner has he stepped off the train and onto the platform than the locomotive—in Isaac Rosenfeld's inspired translation—"lets out a blast and blasts his Passover to pieces."

The story goes on from there, but this decisive sequence of events makes two points about Jewish identity. It is not always a difficult thing to mask—look at the difference a hat makes in how people treat Sholem Shachnah. Not a man's essence but a simple disguise that's easy to effect is what transforms him in the eyes of others. In his own eyes, however, he is a Jew and therefore an impostor, and so he recoils in horror from his mirrored image and takes action "to wake himself up" from whatever it was—a delusion, a fraud, or a dream combining the two.

The motif of the disguised Jew among the gentiles, down to the shocked glance at the mirror, is replicated—though toward an opposite moral—in the blackface scene in *The Jazz Singer*.

In the movie, the first successful talking picture, Jakie Rabinowitz, whose father is forbiddingly bearded and whose Yiddish-speaking mama reads no English, becomes Jack Robin, star of stage, played by Al Jolson, born Asa Yoelson, son of a Lithuanian cantor, who arrived in this country at the age of eight in or around 1894.[25] Jolson belts out some of his favorite songs, "Mammy" and "Blue Skies" among them, and shows off his virtuoso whistling. When he whistles you would swear it was a chorus of birds.

The confusion of actor and role may never have been greater than in *The Jazz Singer*. Jolson, the son of a cantor, plays Jakie Rabinowitz, the son of a cantor (played by Warner Oland, who later played Charlie Chan). As the movie begins the first title card reads: "Perhaps this little plaintive, wailing song of jazz is, after all, the misunderstood utterance of a prayer." Perhaps. And remember, too, that "jazz" in common discourse in America in 1927 connoted a cocktail of Jewish gin and black vermouth.

It is the night of Kol Nidre, the most solemn night in the Hebrew calendar. Mama (Sara Rabinowitz) says, "Maybe our boy doesn't want to be a cantor, Papa." That would break with the tradition of five generations. In a tavern Jakie is singing about his gal Sal, "a sweet sort of devil / But dead on the level." And there is always a Moisha Yudleson to spy and squeal on the high-spirited lad who strays from the path.

The son rebels. "If you whip me again I'll run away and never come back." Years go by. Jakie Rabinowitz has become Jack Robin, singer extraordinaire. "Wait a minute. You ain't heard nothin' yet." Suitable first words for the first talking picture. He sings "Toot, Toot, Tootsie, Goodbye." "There are lots of jazz singers, but you sing with a tear in your voice." And I thought of what Mel Tormé said about Harold Arlen: Unlike many songwriters, who disappoint when singing their own creations, "Arlen sang with great robust ness, in tune, and his voice had a slight cantorial pitch to it that tore at your heart."[6]

In the movie, Jolson plays "Blue Skies" at the piano for Mama. "I'm going to sing it jazzy," he says. Joke: For his sixtieth birthday, the boy's father receives the same present (a prayer shawl) from everyone. The implication is not that the characters lack imagination but that orthodox Judaism is as one-dimensional as it is strict.

Jakie insists that it is "as honorable to sing in a theater as in a temple." That seems to be the film's thesis. Jack Robin and *shiksa* girlfriend Mary Dale star in *April Follies*. Moisha Yudleson, whose part in the action is more complicated than expected, goes backstage, wanting to see Jakie. He is intercepted. "Can't you read?" The sign says NO ADMITTANCE. Yudleson waves it off with a shrug: "Who's smoking?" And this is the fellow who reads the singer's letters to his illiterate Mama!

Yudleson tells Jakie, Tomorrow is Yom Kippur and "they" want you to sing. Your father is very sick. But the show opens tomorrow night. Will you be the first Rabinowitz in five generations to fail God?

The cantor is on his sickbed. If only his son would chant in shul tonight he would win the forgiveness to which each Jewish son is entitled. But tonight is the opening. He can't miss that. But if he doesn't, he will fail his father. What should he do?

And now in his dressing room Jolson puts on blackface and a black toupee. This is his costume but also his mask, donned to find out his true identity or else to conceal its absence. This is who he is: his shadow self, his secret sharer. He is neither one thing nor the other, neither Jew-boy nor red-blooded American, but something else on the cusp of becoming. The "cry of my race" is in his heart. Guilt! Torment! Agony! In blackface he looks in the mirror and sees his father singing in shul. "The songs of Israel are tearing at my heart." But Mary Dale argues in favor of his career. God wants you here—that is, in the theater, she says.

"You're right. My career means more to me than anything in the world."

"More than me?" she asks. He nods. "Then don't let anything stand in your way—not your parents, not me, not anything," she says.

Mama comes to the theater with Yudleson. "Jakie—this ain't you?"

Yudleson says, "He talks like Jakie, but he looks like his shadow." His father is dying. Kol Nidre is two hours away. "Just like his Papa—with the cry in his voice."

"He's not *my* boy anymore—he belongs to the whole world now," his mother says.

The father tells the boy, "My son—I love you."

The boy thinks, "It's a choice between giving up the biggest chance in my life or breaking my mother's heart."

"You must sing tonight."

"I haven't sung Kol Nidre since I was a boy."

"What a little boy learns he never forgets."

Mama tells him, "Do what is in your heart, Jakie."

The producer says, "You're a jazz singer at heart."

There will be no performance of *April Follies* tonight. Tonight our boy sings Kol Nidre, bending the notes just as he does when he sings his songs. Papa dies happy. "Mama, we have our son again." He's "a jazz singer, singing to his god," says Mary Dale. But hello—what's this: Somehow he manages also to sing in *April Follies*. He does so triumphantly, with Mama and Yudleson in the audience. Mammy!

I was talking to Dr. Heinrich Kampf, noted psychiatrist, about Freud's book *The Future of an Illusion*, in which religion is described as an "illusion"; a proper "education in reality" requires a dose of atheism or at least a healthy agnosticism. Somehow the subject of *The Jazz Singer* came up. I acknowledged that Jolson's career as depicted in *The Jazz Singer* is a deviation from the path of tradition, a decisive break in the generations. But (I said) it is a rebellion, not a negation, for he applies to his "jazz" the same "tear in [his] voice" that he shares with his papa and the five generations of Rabinowitzes before them. As the film itself announces at the outset, "Perhaps this little plaintive, wailing song of jazz is, after all, the misunderstood utterance of a prayer."

"Perhaps," Dr. Kampf replied. "A curious word, 'perhaps.' It turns every declaration into a merely theoretical proposition. It's precisely how we hedge our bets in conversation."

"And what does 'precisely' do to a sentence?"

He let this pass. "Don't you sometimes wonder just how satisfactory this has been and is, this attempt to replace religion with art, with culture?" He paused. "With entertainment?"

And what's in a name? This man Yudleson in the movie—what do you think is his significance? Notice that his name begins with the word for Jew in German, Jude. Who is the Yudleson in your life?

The blackface scene may have scared some away from the film, but Gary Giddins is right: "*The Jazz Singer* scrupulously avoids using blackface for comic relief or nostalgia. When Rabinowitz finally 'blacks up' in his dressing room, the effect has a metaphorical purity; he doesn't know who he is, and putting on the wig and cork provides temporary comfort: He smiles at his gentile lover as he puts on the mask that will make him a star even as it renders him invisible. In the end, he is no more himself filling in for his dying father on Kol Nidre [night] than he is in minstrel drag."[27]

Choose one of the following, and elaborate:

1. Jakie, the family's black sheep, has to put on blackface to express his inner self.
2. He is a white man with a black soul.
3. He has to co-opt the African American experience in order to be both expressive and popular.
4. He integrates the black and Jewish musical idioms to achieve something new called jazz, and thus he stands

for the fellowship between Jewish songwriters and black performers.

5. He is the mirror or shadow version of Miles Davis playing "Bess, You Is My Woman Now" or Sarah Vaughan singing "How Long Has This Been Going On?"

6. He is putting on a mask to discover himself in the manner recommended by Oscar Wilde and exemplified by William Butler Yeats and Ezra Pound, who employed masks and personae in their poems.

7. Shades of the biblical Jacob, disguising himself as his brother Esau to win the paternal blessing.

When Jack Robin in blackface says he hears "the cry of my race," the phrase bursts with surplus meaning. What constitutes his race—the color of his skin, the tear in his voice? The movie favors a "both/and" rather than an "either/or" approach. In blackface, Jack can look in the mirror and see his father the cantor wailing in shul; he remains the cantor's son when he blackens his face with burnt cork, and he succeeds onstage, a great American entertainer. And how does he do it? By being black. According to one commentator from the old days, "jazz is the new prayer of the American masses, and Al Jolson is their cantor. The Negro makeup in which he expresses his misery is the appropriate *talis* for such a communal leader."[28]

Here's how the music critic David Schiff made sense of these complex racial interactions in 1997: "While blacks might be lower in the social order than Jews, they were also, by being Christian, at once more American and more religious than the immigrant Jews, many of whom had abandoned any religious practice. African Americans were also more embedded in American history, however tragically, than Jews would ever be. Jewish blackface was thus a complex phase of cultural negotiation which partook of identification and indifference, idealization and condescension, admiration and envy."[29]

A "complex phase of cultural negotiation": This has the ring of a truth, even if only a sociological truth. But is it what the performers themselves thought? And here, as my own last word on the subject, I quote from Arlene Croce's 1965 essay on Fred Astaire in *Swing Time*, "Notes on La Belle, La Perfectly Swell, Romance." Of the dancer's impersonation of "Bojangles of Harlem," Croce writes that "Astaire in blackface, in ragtime hoodoo, stays Astaire, stays white, but the dance he does is not race caricature. It has the dignity of homage."[30]

The real problem with *The Jazz Singer* is not that Jakie Rabinowitz puts on blackface to become Jack Robin. That part I understand. The real problem is that in the abstract debate between alienation and assimilation—between the past, the family, and orthodox Judaism, on the one hand, and the future, the self, and the secular life, on the other—the film has it both ways, and this is not possible. The hero sings Kol Nidre in shul, makes his father happy, and earns his blessing. But he also sings in the theater to his own mammy, who sits thrilled beside Yudleson. He makes no sacrifice. It wasn't a real dilemma. It was no contest. Jack's return to the fold of his father's religion was just a one-night stand of piety. The voice in the back of my head says: So? "So," I answer, "the movie was unreal." "Unreal," the voice echoes. "And since when is reality what you want from the movies?"

If *The Jazz Singer* is a parable of the assimilation of the Jew into American life, it is also a largely accurate depiction of the path taken by Jolson, the cantor's boy who left home to find his true calling as a minstrel. A minstrel: According to Irving Caesar, a minstrel is what a "real lyric-writer" is:

> a fellow who can't help singing, and he sings through his words. A poet or a versifier—they must be satisfied to write their words down. That's all. But a lyricist— he's a *minstrel!* Think how this whole business of popular songs came about—through the old-time minstrel shows. The fellows who sang in those shows needed more songs to sing, and if they could write 'em, they wrote 'em for themselves, and if they could write fast enough, instead of going on the road for ten dollars a week and living in those terrible boardinghouses in small one-horse towns, they learned they could *sell* their songs—for ten dollars or fifteen—and it saved them from going out on the road!"

Dream a little dream of me and I will dream of you. Can't you see we're meant to be a team of two?

If you are but a dream, what am I? No longer a Jew acceptable to his paternity, not quite a fully integrated American citizen but something else, something between them, my own shadow: a masked minstrel who looks in the mirror, sees things that aren't there, then goes out on the stage to perform for the day's required dose of applause, which proves that he exists, praise the Lord.

VIII

Some Other Time

Oh well, it was swell while it lasted.
LEO ROBIN, "Thanks for the Memory"

Yesterdays

Yesterday was November 25, Arthur Schwartz's birthday, so I watched *The Band Wagon* with Fred Astaire dancing and singing "By Myself" and "Put a Shine on Your Shoes" and other songs Schwartz wrote with Howard Dietz as his lyricist. Astaire, Nanette Fabray, and Jack Buchanan are baby triplets in one of the wackiest numbers ever. The day before was November 22, the day Kennedy was killed, also Hoagy Carmichael's birthday, and I watched a bunch of conspiracy films on the History Channel and listened to the baritone Richard Lalli sing "How Little We Know" and realized how great it is—the music by Hoagy Carmichael, the lyrics by Johnny Mercer, born on November 18. Yesterday was November 11, Veterans' Day, the day that Jerome Kern collapsed on the sidewalk and breathed his last, and I listened to the young Sinatra sing "Two Hearts Are Better than One," which the old master wrote with a Mercer lyric. And the day before that was September 26, George Gershwin's birthday, and I went out and played the whole Ella Fitzgerald three-disc Gershwin songbook (arrangements by Nelson Riddle) straight through. If every day is the anniversary of someone who died or was born to lift the soul of man under capitalism or socialism, I say play on. Let music be the food of love and let me feast on the lyrics of Irving Kahal ("When I Take My Sugar to Tea," 1931, music Sammy Fain), Bob Hilliard ("The Coffee Song," c. 1946), and Haven Gillespie ("You Go to My Head," 1928, music J. Fred Coots). I cannot bear to leave unmentioned some vocalists. Nor shall I overlook the songs Carolyn Leigh (née Rosenthal) wrote for Cy Coleman's music. "Witchcraft" (1957) was the perfect Sinatra finger-snapping vehicle. Leigh—born August 21— also wrote the words for the swinging sixties song whose title serves as the optimistic legend on Frank's gravestone: "The Best Is Yet to Come."

Noah Rosenblatt and I are still in touch, still get together once in a while for a martini and a steak, still feel guilty about giving up *kashruth*, still resort to Yiddish for *shiksa* and *gonif, macher* and *nebbish, tsuris* and *bondel*. I talked to him often during the writing of this book. Remember when the media discovered Sandy Koufax's Judaism? I think it was in a *Life* magazine cover story that Koufax was called the "sensible southpaw." Noah says it was there that Koufax explained the difference between a *schlemiel* and a *schlemazel*, the former being the person who spills his glass of milk at a party and the latter the hapless soul on whom the milk is spilled. It's Noah's theory that the lifespan of the American popular song as a current phenomenon, when the material was new and original and not part of a repertory, was approximately fifty years. But this, he hastens to add, is a long time for a cultural movement. Today it exists as a cultural inheritance kept alive by underfunded jazz stations, dedicated disc jockeys, and Woody Allen. Yesterday it was sweeping the nation. What is amazing is how short the life of even the most extraordinary movement may be. Abstract Expressionism, which shifted the global center of gravity from Paris to New York, lasted essentially twenty years before an array of newer movements, many of them forgettable, superseded it in the marketplace and in the calculations of dealers and collectors.

"It all comes together," Noah says. Look at baseball. It was at the height of its prestige and popularity in the early 1950s, and the sport's signature moment remains Bobby Thomson's home run off a Ralph Branca fastball to win the pennant for the Giants against the Dodgers on October 3, 1951. No one knew it at the time, but the culture had peaked. New York had peaked. Think of it: From 1949 through 1964 at least one and sometimes two New York teams played in the World Series every year but one (and in that one exceptional year of 1959, the winning team had formerly played for Brooklyn).[1] When the Dodgers and Giants left Brooklyn and Manhattan for Los Angeles and San Francisco, respectively, in 1957, it was devastating for the city. And in the long run it wasn't all that great for baseball either, although the expansion to new markets was inevitable. Soon enough football supplanted baseball as the national pastime, and eventually, on the sports pages, the games themselves were buried amid matters legal, criminal, financial, medical, and pharmacological. But the loss of the two storied National League franchises, and the death of nightclubs like the Copa or El Morocco, the Stork Club or Café Society, and the decline of jazz, and the devaluing of narrative in fiction and melody in music, and the end of the time when a composer like Harold Arlen could team up with a Ted Koehler or a Yip Harburg—don't you think these things are all connected? I do, Noah, and am glad to credit you here for this observation, which reminds me of that day in 1957, when we went with our fathers, may they rest in peace, to Ebbets Field and saw Koufax pitch and Duke Snider collect his 1,500th hit—a clean line drive, if memory serves.

Through Noah I got back in touch with Amy Grossman, now Amy King. She married a fellow she met at Columbia Business School, and Charles has done very well. He is one of five portfolio managers of a highly successful multicap growth fund that has beaten its benchmark, the S&P 500 Index, for five of the last six years. When I came over for dinner, he showed me a list of the fund's current fifteen largest holdings. Most were familiar names like Coke, Pepsi, UPS, FedEx, Chevron, and Intel. But the largest position by far—more than 5 percent of the fund's total net assets—was in an out-of-the-way company called the Potash Corporation of Saskatchewan, which controls more than 75 percent of the world's excess supply of potash at a moment when the demand for potash is great. "That's the secret," Charles said. "All you need is one. You do all this research on stocks, you employ all these analysts, and all you need is one." Once or twice when I looked at Charles I thought I could imagine myself in his place. His was the road not taken. Amy herself has become a modestly successful author of kosher cookbooks. She loves the old songs as much as I do. Did she have any advice for me as I set out to write this book? Stay away from stating the obvious, she said. Like what? Like belaboring Irving Berlin's "common touch," or Jule Styne's "brassy" sound, or Cole Porter's "sophistication," or how insipid are Otto Harbach's lyrics in "Smoke Gets in Your Eyes" and yet it's not fatal to the song. Dwell instead on Harbach's excellent work on another Kern song, "She Didn't Say Yes." I asked her to name five favorites, and she barely hesitated before she named Jo Stafford and the Pied Pipers singing "Embraceable You" and then an early Billie Holiday recording of "Easy to Love." Three more, I said. Well, she said, there's Ella's cover of a Mercer lyric I know you like, "When a Woman Loves a Man" (music Gordon Jenkins and Bernie Hanighen), and it's hard to beat Johnny Hartman's version of "These Foolish Things," and I'll go out with "Thanks for the Memory" with Benny Goodman's big band and Martha Tilton's voice. You know me, she said. Ever the romantic.

I phoned Robert Pinsky and told him I was writing this book. Robert plays tenor sax, and we talked about movies punctuated by popular songs, as when Lauren Bacall sits on the piano and sings "And Her Tears Flowed Like Wine" (music Stan Kenton and Charles Lawrence, lyrics Joe Greene) at Eddie Mars's casino in *The Big Sleep*. Pinsky, picturing the scene, talked about the nightspots that were common in the old movies. "I thought when you got to be a grown-up, you put on evening clothes and went to a roadhouse where people show up in black tie and there's live music," he said. "From the movies you got a mythology of what grown-up life would be like. You put on really nice clothes and everyone's wearing black tie. There's a live band, cigarette girls, hatcheck girls. I remember thinking, 'When I grow up I'm going to do that.' It was probably an invention of screenwriters just like gunfights where it depends on who shoots fastest." I said that the songs were almost as crucial to the charm of those movies as the clothes or the Warner Brothers cast, and he agreed, saying that the songs are "beautifully designed off-the-rack rather than custom-made daydreams." I said that's a great phrase. Have you used it before? And he said no, that's just the way I talk. The songs are fantasies from the fictionalized first-person point of view. You can imagine you're in a cottage for sale or in Manhattan. Speaking of imagination, I said, I'm writing the book in a way that intermingles fact and fantasy even though it is technically a nonfiction book. That's perfectly in keeping with the fantasy character of the songs themselves, he replied.

When I called Richard Wilbur, he singled out the lyrics of "If I Could Be with You" (music James P. Johnson, lyrics Henry Creamer) and "Paper Moon" (music Harold Arlen, lyrics Yip Harburg) for high praise and recommended Ruth Etting's version of the former. Dick said he loved the internal rhyme of "statue" and "that you" in "Bill," the showstopper that Helen Morgan sang atop a piano in the original version of *Show Boat*.[2] He talked about Leonard Bernstein and about the exhilaration of writing for the theater. When he and Lenny collaborated on *Candide* there were nights they were still writing at four in the morning. How did you get along? "We had a couple of little old storms. He was used to being the whole show. There were moments I strongly questioned that supposition. But neither of us was a good quarreler. We sulked and then got over it. One of us would have a great idea, and we were enthusiastic just as before." Dick told me not to neglect Frank Loesser in my book. Or Cole Porter. Just listen to the way Porter manages all the "I" sounds in "I Get a Kick Out of You." Flying, high, guy, sky, my idea. A few months later I got a card from Dick extending the conversation. "Not long ago, I heard Joan Morris sing Vincent Youmans's 'More Than You Know,' accompanied by William Bolcom on the piano. One line of the lyric [by Edward Eliscu] bowled me over. The first line, 'More than you know,' says that the beloved doesn't know the full extent to which he or she is adored. But the penultimate line suddenly changes everything: 'More than I'd show' turns the whole thing into soliloquy." I hear that the New York City Opera is putting on a new production of *Candide*. You can bet I'll be there.

Why Don't You Run Upstairs and Write a Nice Gershwin Tune?

Today is November 24, 2006. Betty Comden, née Cohen, died yesterday at age eighty-nine. She and her partner Adolph Green wrote *On the Town* and *Wonderful Town* with Leonard Bernstein and *Bells Are Ringing* with Jule Styne. "New York, New York" (the original version goes "The Bronx is up and the Battery's down"), "I Can Cook, Too,"

"Come Up to My Place"—some of these songs aren't in the movie version of *On the Town* because of how suggestive they were considered to be. The best of all of them was "Some Other Time." She could sing, too, and so could Green, and they were in the original production of *On the Town*, which means that they got to harmonize on this most wistful of love songs: "Can't satisfy my craving— / Never have watched you while you're shaving," and then the vow to "catch up some other time" that may never come. I have Jane Monheit singing it right now and will postpone the next paragraph until I hear it through.

I will always associate Betty Comden not only with Green but with the composer of that tune, Lenny, Leonard Bernstein, the skinny boy wonder from Lawrence, Massachusetts, who at the age of twenty-four, on less than a day's notice, conducted the New York Philharmonic in place of an ailing Bruno Walter at Carnegie Hall. It was on a November Sunday in 1943. Without having had the chance to rehearse the music, the substitute conductor amazed the audience and the musicians themselves. "You just couldn't believe a young man could create that kind of music," said the violinist Jacques Margulies, who played in the orchestra that afternoon. "We were supposed to have gone over it with Bruno Walter, we had rehearsed it with him and performed it with him, and this had nothing to do with Bruno Walter. The orchestra stood up and cheered. We were open-mouthed. That man was the most extraordinary musician I have heard in my life."[3]

Bernstein was a second Gershwin, people said, or he should be, and why didn't he write more like George? So many people said roughly the same thing that Lenny felt obliged to answer in the form of a somewhat defensive "imaginary conversation" he reprinted in *The Joy of Music*. He explained that Gershwin had gone from popular music to classical whereas he, Lenny, had done the reverse. "George was just like you, highbrow, one foot in Carnegie Hall and the other in Tin Pan Alley," says the voice in the composer's head, to which his own voice answers: "I wrote a symphony before I ever wrote a popular song. How can you expect me to have that simple touch he had?" In the dialogue, Bernstein makes it plain just how much he loves *Rhapsody in Blue* and *An American in Paris*. Nevertheless he deprecates each as a "study in tunes," great melodies to be sure, but "stuck together—with a thin paste of flour and water." It is with *Porgy and Bess* that Gershwin hit his stride, says Bernstein. "With *Porgy* you suddenly realize that Gershwin was a great, great theater composer. He always had been. Perhaps that's what was wrong with his concert music: It was really theater music thrust into a concert hall. What he would have done in the theater in another ten or twenty years! And then he would still have been a young man! What a loss! Will America realize what a loss it was?"[4] The title Bernstein gave to this "imaginary conversation" is "Why Don't You Run Upstairs and Write a Nice Gershwin Tune?" It's a question Bernstein does as much to evade as to address, but the ecstatic description of Gershwin as a theater composer is telling. Why after *West Side Story* did Bernstein fail to write a great show?

Instead, Lenny got to be the conductor of the New York

Philharmonic. A champion chain-smoker and Scotch-swiller, he composed large-scale works (*Jeremiah*, *The Age of Anxiety*, *Kaddish*), became a media star (*Omnibus*, *Young People's Concerts*), and was constantly in motion working on multiple projects concurrently. Lenny was a genius and he had chutzpah.[5] He wrote the music for *On the Town* and *Wonderful Town* with lyrics by Comden and Green; *Candide* with Dick Wilbur and John LaTouche, Dorothy Parker, Lillian Hellman, and Stephen Sondheim, among others; and *West Side Story* with Sondheim. These are major additions to the Broadway repertory, the last or next-to-last hurrah of the Great White Way. Yet none of Bernstein's accomplishments spared him from sharp criticism, not only from professional naysayers but from that much more difficult-to-please critic, the superego. Like Auden, Lenny had made the unforgivable error of appearing on the scene early and in full glory, a wunderkind destined to become a cultural hero, and thus forever after every public move he made would be held up to scrutiny and judged. It was said that he had squandered his gifts, had pandered to the audience. He was histrionic. He liked being a celebrity too much. Back in 1946 Virgil Thomson in the *New York Herald-Tribune* accused Bernstein of "sheer vainglory." He characterized Bernstein's conducting style as "ostentatious" and "a vehicle for the waving about of hair, for the twisting of shoulders and torso, for the miming by facial expressions of uncontrolled emotional states." Well, maybe Lenny—a man of high self-regard—could laugh or shrug off such carping. But it was harder for him to resist the voice in his head that said that classical music was more serious and important than popular song or musical theater in the manner of Brecht and Weill's *Threepenny Opera* or Rodgers and Hammerstein's *Carousel*.

In *On the Town*, Bernstein commented in 1981, he and his collaborators created "a happy and moving show about wartime, in the lightest possible vein but with a most serious aesthetic means." Something about the show tells the viewer that the writers were having a wonderful time. In her biography of the composer, Joan Peyser reports that he needed an operation (deviated septum in the nose) as did Adolph Green (removal of tonsils) in the summer of 1944, so they scheduled the operations in the same hospital at the same time and shared a room. That room became the temporary center of operations of *On the Town*—"rather like a Marx Brothers movie," Peyser says.[6] That was one side of Lenny: always working, with energy to spare and to share. There was also a darker side, a secret self; his marriage to a Jewish convert could not satisfy his cravings or serve as an effective cover to conceal his homosexual nature. Peyser depicts him as a man torn between rival impulses: "between composing and conducting, between art music and pop, between hetero- and homosexuality."[7]

It would be surprising then if Bernstein was anything but ambivalent about Judaism. Unlike Irving Berlin, Harold Arlen, Vernon Duke (Vladimir Dukelsky), and many others, Bernstein did not change his name.[8] It was an emphatically Jewish name. (In *Citizen Kane* Mankiewicz and Welles emphasize the Jewishness of Kane's managing editor and second in command, played by Everett Sloan, by calling the character "Mr. Bernstein." Kane lodges authority in him despite the disapproval of the anti-Semitic old guard and treats him with respect; "Mr. Bernstein" may be the only major figure without a reason to be angry with Kane.) Leonard Bernstein was obviously Jewish and also legendarily indiscreet. Joan Peyser reasons that his marriage "may have made Bernstein's future career possible" not because it would give him a cover but because of the "positive message" he was sending to the "community of patrons and managers": "You know me, if I am willing to get married, I am willing to behave in every way." Peyser tells us on one page that Felicia Montealegre converted to Judaism before marrying Lenny and on the next page that she tried to convert him to a more socially acceptable or putatively normal way of being. In marrying Bernstein, Felicia "did virtually what her mother had done. She married a Jew whom she found vulgar and then proceeded to try to tone him down. 'Stop being so vulgar, Lenny' was a common reprimand heard in public."[9] If "vulgar" here is partly a euphemism for "Jewish," the attempt was doomed to fail. Gunther Schuller on Bernstein: "It is important to him that a composer is a Jew, that a performer is a Jew. He told me that *Triplum*, my composition, has a Jewish soul. That is meant as a compliment. I am not a Jew. When Lenny says, 'You can almost be Jewish,' that is considered by him to be the most supreme of compliments."[10] On the other hand, Bernstein did write a Roman Catholic mass.

The principal collaborators on his greatest popular triumph, *West Side Story*, were all Jews: Stephen Sondheim wrote the lyrics, Arthur Laurents the book; Jerome Robbins did the choreography and directed. The modern version of *Romeo and Juliet*, as Robbins and Bernstein conceived it, had originally pitted Jewish Capulets and Catholic Montagues. The change to a clash of whites versus Puerto Ricans makes excellent theatrical sense. It also continues the pattern: the Jew who shows himself as something other than who he is. Arthur Laurents's play *Home of the Brave* was about a Jewish soldier in the Pacific during World War II. Anti-Semitism figures crucially in the plot. By the time *Home of the Brave* became a movie (and a brilliant one), the central figure is a black man played by James Edwards, and it is racism that the picture addresses. It is, in a sense, a curious form of blackface that the film's writers, Laurents and Carl Foreman, adopt to fight racial prejudice.

If Leonard Bernstein underestimated the value of his popular music, we needn't follow suit. Would that he had written another *On the Town*, a second *West Side Story*. The fact is, he could do everything—compose and conduct and lecture and teach—and it's with the brilliance of his shows and the charisma of his personality in mind that I will end with a sestina about Lenny that may stand as a tribute to all those great musical geniuses who messed so successfully with Mr. In-Between. I will take my title from "The President Jefferson Sunday Luncheon Party March," a great song from a dismal failure of a show, *1600 Pennsylvania Avenue*, which Bernstein wrote with Alan Jay Lerner (1976):

"The Leonard Bernstein Sunday Luncheon Party Sestina"

How goodly to me are the musicals of Leonard
    Bernstein!
I remember the first time I saw *West Side Story*

(the movie). It filled me with joy, as did *On the Town*
(both the show and the movie). *Wonderful Town*
wowed us at Lincoln Center in 2004. I love Dick Wilbur's
    lyrics for *Candide*,
which is sublime indeed, as is the sound track of *On the*
    Waterfront.

As I wrote that stanza, it occurred to me that the sestina
    is a great front
for the opinions of a partisan of Leonard Bernstein
with a weakness for *1600 Pennsylvania Avenue*, which,
    though inferior to *Candide*,
has the great "President Jefferson Sunday Luncheon
    Party March." The story
of the three sailors in New York for a day (in *On the*
    Town)
is better than that of the Ohio sisters in Greenwich
    Village (in *Wonderful Town*).

Few songs are as great as "Some Other Time" in *On the*
    Town,
1944 version. On TV today I saw *On the Waterfront*.
Without the music would the story
move us as it does? I doubt it. Bernstein,
a lover of the city, may have lacked the optimism of
    Candide
yet captured the naïve confidence of his musical town.

As Cole Porter would say, Get out of town!
New York town!

where caustic critics are candid
but may have nothing behind their front
and should spend more time listening to Leonard
    Bernstein
conduct Mahler or teach schoolkids with the confidence
    of a lover in a story

in that rarest of literary creations, a story
with a happy ending, taking place in a town
that exists in a dream where Bernstein
sits at the piano of his town
house while we stand in front
of the open window, listening like Candide

to Pangloss in the best of all possible versions of *Candide.*
The sestina form can serve as a vehicle for a story.
The sestina may even be a front
for a story. And that story concerns a town,
not *Our Town,*
but New York City in the mind of Leonard Bernstein.

So here's to you, Leonard Bernstein,
and your music in *On the Town, On the Waterfront,*
Candide, Wonderful Town, and *West Side Story.*

CHRONOLOGY

c. 1000 BCE   King David, a musician to whom the Book of Psalms is traditionally attributed, rules over the Kingdom of Israel.

1654   Twenty-three Jews, the first to settle in North America, arrive in New Amsterdam from Recife, Brazil.

1763   Congregation Yeshuat Yisrael in Newport, Rhode Island, dedicates its famed home, known as the Touro Synagogue, after its then cantor, Isaac Touro.

1818   The Hamburg Temple, an early Reform synagogue, opens and features organ playing on Shabbat.

1835   *La Juive*, an opera by French Jewish composer Fromental Halévy, premieres. The story of a Jewess who falls in love with a gentile man becomes a popular part of opera repertoire for more than one hundred years.

1863   Oscar Hammerstein I, age sixteen, arrives in New York from Germany; he becomes a builder of opera houses in America.

1871   *Thespis*, the first collaboration by W. S. Gilbert and Arthur Sullivan, kicks off the genre of light opera, a precursor of the theatrical musical.

1881   The assassination of Czar Alexander II in Russia is followed by waves of pogroms and the massive emigration of Russian Jews to the United States.

1885   Jerome Kern is born in New York City to a German Jewish father and an American-born Austrian Jewish mother.

1886   Gus Kahn is born in Germany.

1888   Irving Berlin is born in Kirghizia, Russia, to a cantor father.

1894   Ted Koehler is born in Washington, D.C.

1895   Oscar Hammerstein II, grandson of Oscar Hammerstein I, is born in New York City.

1896   Ira Gershwin is born in New York City.

Howard Dietz is born in New York City.

1898   Yip Harburg is born to Orthodox Jewish parents in New York City.

George Gershwin is born in Brooklyn.

1900   Leo Robin is born in Pittsburgh.

Arthur Schwartz is born in Brooklyn.

1902   Richard Rodgers is born in New York City.

1903 Vladimir Dukelsky, who would write songs under the name Vernon Duke, is born in Russia.

1905 Dorothy Fields is born in Allenhurst, New Jersey; her father is comedian Lew Fields.

Harold Arlen is born in Buffalo, New York.

Jule Styne is born in London; he later emigrates with his family to Chicago.

1910 Frank Loesser is born in New York City.

Jerome Kern's first Broadway show, *Mr. Wix of Wickham*, premieres.

1911 Irving Berlin has his first major success with "Alexander's Ragtime Band."

1913 Sammy Cahn is born in New York City to Galician immigrant parents.

1914 Jerome Kern writes the music for the song "They Didn't Believe Me," considered by many to be the first modern American song, for the musical *The Girl from Utah*.

June 28, 1914 The assassination of Austrian Archduke Franz Ferdinand, which will spark World War I.

1917 Richard Rodgers sees the Columbia Varsity Show, meets Hammerstein backstage, and decides he wants to go to Columbia and write the Varsity Show.

1918   Leonard Bernstein is born in Lawrence, Massachusetts.

1919   George Gershwin has a hit with "Swanee," sung by Al Jolson.

1924   George Gershwin writes *Rhapsody in Blue.*

George and Ira Gershwin write *Lady, Be Good!* their first Broadway musical.

1925   Rodgers and Hart score big on Broadway with the song "Manhattan," in the revue *Garrick Gaieties.*

1926   Richard Rodgers meets Cole Porter in Venice.

1927   *The Jazz Singer,* the first motion picture with synchronized music and dialogue, opens; it tells the story of a cantor's son who leaves his Orthodox Jewish family to sing jazz.

The musical *Show Boat,* with music by Jerome Kern and lyrics by Oscar Hammerstein II, premieres on Broadway.

1928   Eddie Cantor sings "Makin' Whoopee" in the musical *Whoopee!,* with music by Walter Donaldson and lyrics by Gus Kahn.

The *Threepenny Opera,* with music by Kurt Weill and text by Bertolt Brecht, is first performed in Berlin.

1929   The song "I Guess I'll Have to Change My Plan," music by Arthur Schwartz and lyrics by Howard Dietz, is featured in the revue *The Little Show.*

October 1929   The stock market crash heralds the beginning of the Great Depression.

1930   Stephen Sondheim is born in New York City.

1931   Yip Harburg writes the lyrics to the Depression anthem "Brother, Can You Spare a Dime?" with music by Jay Gorney.

Herman Hupfield writes the words and music of "As Time Goes By," the song that the Ingrid Bergman and Humphrey Bogart characters will ask "Sam" to play in *Casablanca* (1942).

1932   Duke Ellington composes "It Don't Mean a Thing (If It Ain't Got That Swing)." The swing era will commence in earnest in 1935.

Of Thee I Sing, with a score by the Gershwin brothers, becomes the first musical to win a Pulitzer Prize.

1933   Harold Arlen and Ted Koehler write "Stormy Weather" for the *Cotton Club Revue*.

October 10, 1935   *Porgy and Bess*, by George and Ira Gershwin with DuBose Heyward, premieres on Broadway with an all African American cast.

1935   The Benny Goodman Trio breaks the color barrier with Teddy Wilson at the piano.

1936   Jerome Kern and Dorothy Fields win an Academy Award for the song "The Way You Look Tonight" from the movie *Swing Time*.

July 11, 1937   George Gershwin dies suddenly at age thirty-eight.

November 2, 1937   Broadway premiere of *I'd Rather Be Right*, a satirical Rodgers and Hart show about Franklin Delano Roosevelt.

1937   Sammy Cahn, with Saul Chaplin, writes English lyrics for "Bei Mir Bist Du Schoen," based on a 1932 Yiddish musical; it becomes a number-one hit for the Andrews Sisters.

1938   Nazi Germany annexes Austria.

November 9–10, 1938   Kristallnacht, a Nazi-sponsored pogrom, devastates the Jewish communities of Germany and Austria.

November 11, 1938   Kate Smith sings Irving Berlin's "God Bless America" on her radio show.

1939   *The Wizard of Oz* is released; the film will go on to win the Academy Award for Best Original Song for "Over the Rainbow," by Harold Arlen and Yip Harburg.

1940   Rodgers and Hart's *Pal Joey* opens on Christmas Day.

1942   Irving Berlin writes "White Christmas."

Frank Loesser, while serving in the Radio Productions Unit during World War II, writes the hit song "Praise the Lord and Pass the Ammunition."

March 31, 1943   Crematorium II opens at Auschwitz.

March 31, 1943   *Oklahoma!* the first Rodgers and Hammerstein musical, premieres.

November 14, 1943   Leonard Bernstein conducts the New York Philharmonic in a last-minute substitution for conductor Bruno Walter.

November 22, 1943   Lorenz Hart dies in New York of pneumonia.

1944   Leonard Bernstein composes the music for *On the Town*, with lyrics by Betty Comden and Adolph Green.

Frank Sinatra sings "Ol' Man River" at the Hollywood Bowl, bringing MGM mogul Louis B. Mayer to tears.

April 19, 1945 *Carousel*, by Rodgers and Hammerstein, opens on Broadway.

1945 World War II ends.

Mel Tormé and Robert Wells write "The Christmas Song."

The Frank Sinatra short "The House I Live In," by Albert Maltz, Earl Robinson, and Abel Meeropol, wins an honorary Oscar.

Jerome Kern dies.

1946 Irving Berlin's Broadway hit *Annie Get Your Gun* opens.

MGM releases a biopic on the life of Jerome Kern, *Till the Clouds Roll By*, starring Robert Walker as Kern.

Mel Tormé sings on Artie Shaw's album of Cole Porter's music.

1947 Leonard Bernstein conducts the Palestine Orchestra, soon to become the Israel Philharmonic Orchestra.

May 14, 1948 The founding of the State of Israel.

April 7, 1949   Rodgers and Hammerstein's *South Pacific* premieres on Broadway.

December 8, 1949   *Gentlemen Prefer Blondes*, music by Jule Styne and lyrics by Leo Robin, premieres on Broadway.

September 21, 1950   Frank Sinatra records "Meet Me at the Copa" (Sammy Cahn and Axel Stordahl).

November 24, 1950   *Guys and Dolls*, music and lyrics by Frank Loesser, premieres on Broadway.

March 29, 1951   Rodgers and Hammerstein's *The King and I* premieres on Broadway.

1953   Leonard Bernstein composes music for *Wonderful Town*, with lyrics by Betty Comden and Adolph Green.

Vincente Minelli's movie *The Bandwagon*, with songs by Arthur Schwartz (music) and Howard Dietz (lyrics), opens.

March 15, 1956   *My Fair Lady*, music by Frederick Loewe and lyrics by Alan Jay Lerner, opens on Broadway.

1956   Ella Fitzgerald records songbooks devoted to Rodgers and Hart and Cole Porter.

September 26, 1957   *West Side Story*, music by Leonard Bernstein, lyrics by Stephen Sondheim, book by Arthur Laurents, and choreography by Jerome Robbins, opens on Broadway.

1958   Miles Davis records Gershwin's *Porgy and Bess*, with orchestra under the direction of Gil Evans.

May 21, 1959   *Gypsy*, starring Ethel Merman, with music by Jule Styne, lyrics by Stephen Sondheim, book by Arthur Laurents, and choreography by Jerome Robbins, opens on Broadway.

1960   Oscar Hammerstein dies.

1962   *How to Succeed in Business Without Really Trying*, music and lyrics by Frank Loesser, wins a Tony Award and Pulitzer Prize.

Bob Dylan releases his first album.

September 22, 1964   *Fiddler on the Roof*, music by Jerry Bock and lyrics by Sheldon Harnick, opens on Broadway.

1964   Ella Fitzgerald records the Johnny Mercer songbook, last in a series that also included Irving Berlin, Duke

Ellington, George and Ira Gershwin, Harold Arlen, and Jerome Kern.

July 25, 1965   Bob Dylan "goes electric" at the Newport Folk Festival, heralding a new musical era.

NOTES

Prelude: Jewish Genius

1. The non-Jewish songwriter is Cole Porter: "The more 'Jewish' he got, the better his music." Wilfrid Sheed, *The House That George Built* (New York: Random House, 2007), p. 153.

2. John Lahr, "Come Rain or Come Shine: The Bittersweet Life of Harold Arlen," *The New Yorker*, September 19, 2005, p. 89.

3. Howard Pollack, *George Gershwin: His Life and Work* (Berkeley: University of California Press, 2006), p. 171.

4. Carolyn Leigh's lyric for "How Little We Know (How Little It Matters)" contains this working definition of "romance": It's what happens "when two tingles intermingle."

5. The lyricists responsible for the songs referred to here are, in order, Oscar Hammerstein, Ira Gershwin, Dorothy Fields, Leo Robin, and Lorenz Hart. "Our romance won't end on a sorrowful note" is the first line of the verse of "They Can't Take That Away from Me." "I know that music leads the way to romance" is from "I Won't Dance."

6. Quoted in Samuel Marx and Jan Clayton, *Rodgers and Hart: Bewitched, Bothered, and Bedeviled* (New York: Putnam, 1976), p. 232.

7. Arlene Croce, "Notes on La Belle, La Perfectly Swell, Romance," in Robert Gottlieb, ed., *Reading Dance* (New York: Pantheon, 2008), p. 64.

8. George Bernard Shaw, *The New Statesman*, March 23, 1962.

9. Pollack, *George Gershwin*, p. 180.

10. Ibid., p. 605.

11. Quoted in ibid., pp. 49–50.

12. Richard Rodgers, *Musical Stages* (1975; repr., New York: Da Capo Press, 2002), p. 88.

13. Of the quintet of Arlen, Berlin, Gershwin, Kern, and Rodgers, the

first three sound most "Jewish," and it can't be an accident that all three came from Eastern European families who fled Russia to escape the murderous pogroms, widespread persecution, and punitive laws such as the mandatory twenty-five-year hitch in the military, all of which followed the assassination of a liberal czar in 1881.

14. Pollack, *George Gershwin*, pp. 46, 237.

15. Music and lyrics by Bert Kalmar and Harry Ruby.

16. Depending on context, one can translate *nu* as "so" (declarative or interrogative), "so what," "all right," and even "let's do it." See William Grimes, "Language of Variety (and Oy, the Insults!)," *New York Times*, October 17, 2007. Review of *Just Say Nu: Yiddish for Every Occasion (When English Just Won't Do)* by Michael Wex (New York: St. Martin's Press, 2007). A Yiddish translation of "The Love Song of J. Alfred Prufrock," translated back into English, begins, "Nu, come on, me and you."

17. Andrea Most, *Making Americans: Jews and the Broadway Musical* (Cambridge, Mass.: Harvard University Press, 2004), p. 107. According to Most, the name Ali Hakim may derive from the Hebrew word *hacham*, or "wise man." Hammerstein referred to himself as "Mister Ali Hakimstein" in the invitation to the first-anniversary party for the show (pp. 113–14).

18. In *Making Americans*, Andrea Most explores at length the idea that musical comedies could allegorically dramatize the assimilation of the Jews. Most characterizes Broadway musicals as "narratives of a desperate Jewish desire to resist essentialized (or racialized) identity through the powerful language of theatricality" (p. 10). The musicals of such as Rodgers and Hammerstein, Rodgers and Hart, and Berlin are, she writes, celebrations of "the marvelous freedom Jews felt in America to invent themselves anew."

I. My Romance

1. The movie has a fine time at the aristocracy's expense. A viscount explains why he ranks lower than dukes and earls: "We got gypped in the Crusades."

2. A variation of this rhyme occurs in *Love Me Tonight* ("Bonjour Monsieur Cohen / How are things go-en?").

3. See Douglas Martin, "Andree de Jongh, 90, of Belgian Resistance," *New York Times*, October 18, 2007.

4. See Karl Frucht, "We Were a P.W.I. Team," *Commentary* (January 1946), pp. 69–76.

5. *Fiddler on the Roof* (music Jerry Bock, lyrics Sheldon Harnick).

6. Frank Loesser wrote the words and music of "Standing on the Corner" (from his musical *The Most Happy Fella*, 1956); Sammy Cahn contributed the lyrics and Jimmy Van Heusen the music for "Love and Marriage" (written for Frank Sinatra to sing in a television version of Thornton Wilder's *Our Town*); Irving Berlin wrote the words and music for "There's No Business Like Show Business" for *Annie Get Your Gun* (1946). Alone among the composers and lyricists just named, Van Heusen (born Edward Chester Babcock of Methodist parents in Syracuse, New York) was not Jewish. Babcock named himself after the Van Heusen shirt, thinking it was a touchstone of old money, elegance, and class. What he didn't realize is that the Van Heusen line was the creation of a German-Jewish peddler named Israel Phillips.

7. Though not in the original Broadway show in 1933, "Lovely to Look At" (lyrics Dorothy Fields) was added to the movie version of *Roberta* and to stage revivals.

8. Edward Jablonski, *Harold Arlen: Happy with the Blues* (New York: (Doubleday, 1961), p. 138.

II. Tales of the Uncles, Part I

1. Barbara Tuchman, *The Guns of August* (1962; repr. New York: Bantam, 1976), p. 489.

2. Sheed, *The House That George Built*, p. 125.

3. An alternative version of these lyrics appears in Charles Schwartz, *Cole Porter: A Biography* (New York: Dial Press, 1979), p. 52, and Mark Steyn, *Broadway Babies Say Goodnight: Musicals Then and Now* (London: Faber and Faber, 1997), p. 41.

4. Guy Bolton, in "Recollections of Jerome Kern," published in *The New York Times* a week after Kern's death, recalls how he "had planned to take the *Lusitania* with Charles Frohman—who so admired his talent—and only missed sailing by having an alarm clock miraculously stop in the night" (*New York Times*, November 18, 1945). Nevertheless, "those that were closest to Kern at the time, including his wife, insist that this story simply has no basis in fact. Kern had no plans whatsoever to go to England with Frohman, and never intended sailing on the *Lusitania*," writes David Ewen in *The World of Jerome Kern* (New York: Henry Holt, 1960), p. 53. More recently, Gerald Bordman tells us that Kern's daughter Betty "definitely recalls both parents confirming the story" and that given the composer's "odd hours," it was entirely plausible that he may have slept too late for the ship's departure at noon, which "Jerry would consider an unsociably early sailing hour." Gerald Bordman, *Jerome Kern: His Life and Music* (New York: Oxford University Press, 1980), pp. 113–14.

5. Kurt List, "Jerome Kern and American Operetta: He Wedded American Lyrique and American Vaudeville," *Commentary* (May 1947), p. 435.

6. Hugh Fordin, *Getting to Know Him: The Biography of Oscar Hammerstein II* (New York: Random House, 1977), p. 126. *Messer Marco Polo* was the name of the story.

7. The New York College of Music was eventually assimilated into New York University.

8. *New York Times*, November 18, 1945.

9. Alan Dale writing in the *American*. Quoted in David Ewen, *Panorama of American Popular Music* (Englewood Cliffs, N.J.: Prentice-Hall, 1957), p. 172.

10. With his brother Weedon, the elder George Grossmith wrote the comic novel *The Diary of a Nobody*, which was published in London in 1892.

11. William G. Hyland, *The Song Is Ended: Songwriters and American Music, 1900–1950* (New York: Oxford University Press, 1995) pp. 36–37.

12. Pollack, *George Gershwin*, p. 84.

13. From an interview with Robert Kimball and Alfred Simon, in *Composers' Voices from Ives to Ellington: An Oral History of American Music*, ed. Vivian Perlis and Libby Van Cleve (New Haven, Conn: Yale University Press, 2005), pp. 216–17.

14. *Composers' Voices*, p. 197.

15. "Thus Kern was willing to limit himself—as Gershwin and Rodgers were not—to the poverty of Broadway and Hollywood." List, "Jerome Kern and American Operetta," p. 438.

16. Max Wilk, *They're Playing Our Song* (New York: Da Capo Press, 1997), p. 134.

17. List, "Jerome Kern and American Operetta," p. 434.

18. Wilk, *They're Playing Our Song*, p. 39.

19. Pollack, *George Gershwin*, p. 95.

20. Croce, "Notes on La Belle, La Perfectly Swell, Romance," pp. 62–63.

21. Deborah Winer, *On the Sunny Side of the Street: The Life and Lyrics of Dorothy Fields* (New York: Schirmer Books, 1997), p. 144.

22. Ibid., p. 27.

23. Ibid., p. 97.

24. See David Lehman, "Frankophilia," *American Heritage* (November-December).

25. See *New York Times*, August 30, 1951.

26. James Van Heusen and Johnny Burke came up with two terrific contenders: "Swinging on a Star" and "Aren't You Glad You're You?"

III. Tales of the Uncles, Part II

1. Wilk, *They're Playing Our Song*, p. 144.

2. John Lahr, "Come Rain or Come Shine," *The New Yorker*, September 19, 2005, p. 90.

3. Jablonski, *Harold Arlen*, p. 38.

4. Ibid., p. 120.

5. Pollack, *George Gershwin*, p. 161.

6. According to Jablonski's *Harold Arlen*, this sequence of events occurred to Arlen in a taxi. The driver was whistling "Stormy Weather."

7. Sheed, *The House That George Built*, p. 9.

8. Jablonski, *Harold Arlen*, p. 68.

9. Sheed, *The House That George Built*, pp. 91, 93.

10. Pollack, *George Gershwin*, p. 162

11. Laurence Bergreen, *As Thousands Cheer: The Life of Irving Berlin* (New York: Penguin, 1990), pp. 167–68, 336–37.

12. "Having learned at some point that the Fieldses were to get only 4 percent of the gross, Berlin asked the astonished producers to reduce his portion by half a percent and add the difference to theirs: 4½ percent for the libretto, and the same for the score." Edward Jablonski, *Irving Berlin: American Troubador* (New York: Henry Holt, 1999), p. 238.

13. W. J. Weatherby, "Irving Berlin: Full Score and One Key," *The Guardian*, September 25, 1989.

14. Robert Kimball, ed., *Cole Porter: Selected Lyrics* (Library of America, 2006), p. 56. A second parody of "You're the Top" was written by Sammy Cahn for Sinatra to sing at a Friars Club dinner in Dean Martin's honor in 1958. An excerpt: "He's the wop! Unlike any other! / He's the wop, who's a mother's mother. / When they split, rumors started spinning; / Full of shit! Dino's just beginning!" The "split" refers to the breakup between Martin and his long-standing partner in comedy, Jerry Lewis. See *Dino: Living High in the Dirty Business of Dreams* by Nick Tosches (New York: Doubleday, 1992), p. 319.

15. Sheed, *The House That George Built*, p. 14.

16. Mary Ellin Barrett, *Irving Berlin: A Daughter's Memoir* (New York: Simon and Schuster, 1994), p. 72.

17. "Harry, Hoagy, and Harold," program notes for the New York Festival of Song, Weill Recital Hall of Carnegie Hall, February 5 and 7, 2008, p. 6.

18. Alec Wilder, *American Popular Song* (1972; repr., New York: Oxford University Press, 1990), pp. 122, 157, 221, 252, 253.

19. Philip Furia, *Ira Gershwin: The Art of the Lyricist* (New York: Oxford University Press, 1996), p. 10.

20. Jablonski, *Harold Arlen*, pp. 120–21.

21. "Who could ask for anything more?" is a key line in both "I Got Rhythm" and "Nice Work If You Can Get It."

22. Gene Lees, *Portrait of Johnny: The Life of John Herndon Mercer* (New York: Pantheon, 2004) p. 186.

23. Jablonski, *Harold Arlen*, pp. 50, 59, 88.

IV. Last Night When We Were Young

1. From Ira's contribution to the memorial volume for his late brother, *George Gershwin*, ed. Merle Armitage (repr., New York: Da Capo Press, 1995), pp. 16–17.

2. Pollack, *George Gershwin*, p. 153.

3. Ibid., p. 110.

4. Ibid., p. 112.

5. Bergreen, *As Thousands Cheer*, p. 347.

6. Ira Gershwin, *Lyrics on Several Occasions* (New York: Knopf, 1959), p. 48.

7. Arthur Loesser, *Men, Women, and Pianos: A Social History* (New York: Simon and Schuster, 1954), pp. 599–608.

8. Thomas L. Riis, *Frank Loesser* (New Haven, Conn.:Yale University Press, 2008), p. 228.

9. Vincent Youmans wrote *Hit the Deck* with lyrics by Leo Robin and Clifford Grey, Rodgers and Hart wrote *A Connecticut Yankee*, the Gershwin Brothers turned out *Funny Face*, and Kern and Hammerstein were responsible for *Show Boat*.

10. If you worked on Wall Street in 1950, you wore suits made by Rogers Peet, Brooks Brothers, or Hart Schaffner & Marx.

11. In a ten-year period in which Porter's *Kiss Me Kate*, Rodgers and Hammerstein's *South Pacific*, Lerner and Loewe's *My Fair Lady*, and Bernstein and Sondheim's *West Side Story* had their runs, I join Sheed in feeling that *Guys and Dolls* is a singular achievement. A couple of the others may have superior scores, but *Guys and Dolls* is "nothing less than the great *New York* musical and the most brilliant evocation ever of the city where songs and shows and so many of the writers came from." It is the epitome of a Broadway show because it is so vividly *of* the very place that produced it and because it is content to *be* what it is—to observe the rules of the genre. See Sheed, *The House That George Built*, p. 272.

12. Sammy Cahn, *I Should Care: The Sammy Cahn Story* (New York: Arbor House, 1970), p. 21. To give you an idea of the alleged inferiority of the *Galitzianer*, consider this excerpt from a 1906 letter sent by "a girl from Galicia" to the editor of New York's Yiddish newspaper, the *Jewish Daily Forward*.

In the shop where I work I sit near a Russian Jew with whom I was always on good terms. Why should one worker resent another?

But once, in a short debate, he stated that all Galicians were no good. When I asked him to repeat it, he answered that he wouldn't retract a word, and that he wished all Galician Jews dead.

I was naturally not silent in the face of such a nasty expression. He maintained that only Russian Jews are fine and intelligent. According to him, the *Galitzianer* are inhuman savages, and he had the right to speak of them so badly.

Dear Editor, does he really have a right to say this? Have the Galician Jews not sent enough money for the unfortunate sufferers of the pogroms in Russia? When a Gentile speaks badly of Jews, it's immediately printed in the newspapers and discussed hotly everywhere. But that a Jew should express himself so about his own brothers is nothing? Does he have a right? Are Galicians really so bad? And does he, the fine Russian, remain fine and intelligent in spite of such expressions?

Isaac Metzker, ed., *A Bintel Brief: Sixty Years of Letters from the Lower East Side to the Jewish Daily* Forward (New York: Schocken, 1971), pp. 58–59.

13. Cahn, *I Should Care*, p. 59.

14. Ibid., pp. 75, 149.

15. Ibid., p. 67.

16. Wilk, *They're Playing Our Song*, p. 172.

17. Ibid., pp. 154–57.

18. Wilder, *American Popular Song*, p. 289.

19. Will Friedwald, *Sinatra! The Song Is You* (New York: Scribner, 1995), p. 55.

20. Jesse Green, "Tolstoy Was Right: Flop Musicals Are All Unique," *New York Times*, April 8, 2007.

21. Jo Stafford interviewed by Bill Redd, *Songbirds*, Winter 2000 www.mrlucky.com/songbirds/html/aug99/9908_stafford.html.

22. Gene Lees, *Portrait of Johnny* (New York: Pantheon, 2004), p. 297.

23. Robert Gottlieb, "Wake Up and Dream," *The New York Review of Books*, August 16, 2007, p. 16. Gottlieb has himself done tremendous service to the American songbook. Together with Robert Kimball, he edited the anthology *Reading Lyrics* (Pantheon, 2000), one of three books that I regard as indispensable. The other two are Alec Wilder's study of American popular song and Max Wilk's book of interviews with songwriters.

24. See David Jenness and Don Velsey, *Classic American Popular Song: The Second Half-Century, 1950–2000* (New York: Routledge, 2006).

V. I Didn't Know What Time It Was

1. Bob Dylan, *Chronicles: Volume One* (New York: Simon and Schuster, 2004), p. 126.

2. Ibid., p. 49.

3. The major Broadway composers fall into three categories: those who wrote the words as well as the music (Irving Berlin, Frank Loesser, Cole Porter, Stephen Sondheim); those who collaborated primarily with one or two partners (George Gershwin, Richard Rodgers); and those who worked with many (Harold Arlen, Cy Coleman, Jerome Kern, Jule Styne).

4. Meryle Secrest, *Somewhere for Me: A Biography of Richard Rodgers* (New York: Applause, 2001), pp. 102, 359.

5. Frederick Nolan, *Lorenz Hart: A Poet on Broadway* (New York: Oxford University Press, 1994), p. 15.

6. "Now, this whole business of integration is a tough one. It demands that a song come out of the situation in the story and make sense with the given characters. In a way, the whole growth of our musical comedy can be seen through the growth of integration." See Leonard Bernstein, *The Joy of Music* (New York: Simon and Schuster, 1959), p. 164.

7. Secrest, *Somewhere for Me*, p. 117.

8. Eleanor Wilner in *First Loves*, ed. Carmela Ciuraru (New York: Scribner, 2000), pp. 247–48.

9. See *The Best American Poetry 2007*, ed. Heather McHugh (New York: Scribner, 2007), pp. 61–62.

10. James Maher, "Introduction," in Wilder, *American Popular Song*, pp. xxv–xxvi.

11. Most, *Making Americans*, pp. 10–11.

12. Philip Furia, *The Poets of Tin Pan Alley* (New York: Oxford University Press, 1992), pp. 9–10.

13. I was about to cite "There Is Nothing Like a Dame" as so intrinsic to *South Pacific* that only in its stage performance can you savor it fully—but I just heard Dick Hyman's piano version, and I take it back.

14. Furia, *The Poets of Tin Pan Alley*, p. 5.

15. Mel Tormé, *My Singing Teachers: Reflections on Singing Popular Music* (New York: Oxford University Press, 1994), p. 112.

16. Secrest, *Somewhere for Me*, pp. 299–300.

17. Rodgers, *Musical Stages*, p. 103.

18. Hyland, *The Song Is Ended*, p. 289.

19. David Ewen, *Richard Rodgers* (New York: Henry Holt, 1957), p. 29.

20. Mary Rodgers, "Introduction," in Richard Rodgers, *Musical Stages*, p. vii.

21. Ewen, *Richard Rodgers*, p. 29.

22. Kitty Kelley, *His Way: The Unauthorized Biography of Frank Sinatra* (New York: Bantam, 1987), pp. 165–66.

23. Remarks during "Harry, Hoagy, and Harold," a concert recital of the New York Festival of Song at Carnegie Hall's Weill Recital Hall, February 7, 2008.

24. Edward Mendelson, *Late Auden* (New York: Farrar, Straus and Giroux, 1999), p. xvii.

VI. The World on a String

1. Jerome Kern, "Tribute" (1938), in *The George Gershwin Reader*, ed. Robert Wyatt and John Andrew Johnson (New York: Oxford University Press, 2004), p. 280.

2. William G. Hyland, *George Gershwin: A New Biography* (Westport, Conn.: Praeger, 2003), p. 215.

3. "Jazz Is the Voice of the American Soul," in *The George Gershwin Reader*, p. 94.

4. Hyland, *The Song Is Ended*, pp. 103, 108.

5. Hyland, *George Gershwin*, p. 216.

6. Jonathan Schwartz, *All in Good Time: A Memoir* (New York: Random House, 2004), pp. 108–9

7. See Kurt List, "George Gershwin's Music: The Greatest American Composer—Alas!" *Commentary* (December 1945), pp. 27, 29, 33.

8. Mr. List may not have been aware of Henry Ford's anti-Semitic tirades collected and published under the title *The International Jew* (1922). Ford was considered a genuine American folk hero, and in an early song Gershwin wrote for the show *Sweet Little Devil* (1924), the Buddy DeSylva lyric rhymes the automaker's name with "our Lord." As for Garbo, in 1930 and 1931 the Gershwin brothers and Ira's wife, Leonore, rented a Beverly Hills house in which Garbo had lived. "Gershwin joked that the fact that he was sleeping in Garbo's bed kept him up some nights" (Pollack, *George Gershwin*, p. 195).

9. See Leo Rosten, *The Joys of Yiddish* (McGraw Hill, 1968; repr., New York: Pocket Books, 1970), p. 93.

10. A. O. Scott, "Another Side of Bob Dylan, and Another, and Another . . ." *New York Times*, November 21, 2007, p. E1.

11. Cahn, *I Should Care*, p. 250.

12. Ibid.

13. Friedwald, *Sinatra!* p. 155.

14. Tormé, *My Singing Teachers*, pp. 117–18, 133–34, 138.

15. "Love Is Just Around the Corner" (1934). Lyrics by Leo Robin, music by Lewis E. Gensler.

16. Tormé, *My Singing Teachers*, p. 66.

17. Jody Rosen, *White Christmas* (New York: Scribner, 2002), p. 23.

18. Gershom Scholem, "Jews and Germans," in *On Jews and Judaism in Crisis: Selected Essays*, ed. Werner J. Dannhauser (New York: Schocken Books, 1976), p. 78.

19. Ibid., p. 83.

20. Ibid., pp. 89–90.

21. Philip Roth, *Operation Shylock: A Confession* (New York: Simon and Schuster, 1993), p. 157.

Notes

22. George S. Kaufman and Moss Hart wrote the book for *I'd Rather Be Right*, a satirical show about President Roosevelt, with score by Richard Rodgers and Lorenz Hart. See *Our Musicals, Ourselves*, by John Bush Jones (Waltham, Mass.: Brandeis University Press, 2003), p. 214.

23. "The steerage passengers would go onto the deck, wanting to drink in their first impressions of their new home. George Gershwin's father leaned out so far his hat flew off in the breeze. He had tucked the name of the family's only contact in America inside that hat." From Lawrence J. Epstein, *At the Edge of a Dream: The Story of Jewish Immigrants on New York's Lower East Side, 1880–1920* (San Francisco: Jossey-Bass, 2007).

24. Sinatra sang the song in the White House more than once: at JFK's inaugural ball in 1961 and again years later when Nixon was the incumbent.

25. Meeropol wrote a stanza in which "black and white" live together, and was incensed when the stanza was not included in the movie.

26. Alfred Kazin, *New York Jew* (New York: Vintage, 1979), p. 15.

27. Ibid., p. 284.

28. Robert Waite, *The Psychopathic God: Adolf Hitler* (New York: Basic Books, 1977), p. 343. Quoted in Charles Lindholm, *Charisma* (Cambridge, Mass.: Basil Blackwell, 1990), p. 102.

29. Anthony Read and David Fisher, *Kristallnacht* (New York: Random House, 1989), p. 7.

30. Philip Furia, *Irving Berlin: A Life in Song* (New York: Schirmer, 1998), p. 195.

31. The practice continues in some places; others have reverted to the deliberately unsolemn "Take Me Out to the Ballgame."

32. See Barrett, *Irving Berlin*, p. 173; and Furia, *Irving Berlin*, pp. 195–97.

33. Furia, *Irving Berlin*, pp. 196–97.

34. Barrett, *Irving Berlin*, p. 122.

35. Ibid., pp. 124, 173.

36. Theodor Reik, *Jewish Wit* (New York: Gamut Press, 1962), p. 90.

VII. A Right to Sing the Blues

1. Rosen, *White Christmas*, p. 12.

2. Robert Alter, "Sentimentalizing the Jews," *Commentary*, September 1965, pp. 71–75.

3. Rodgers, *Musical Stages*, p. 4. Dorothy Rodgers described herself and her husband as "social Jews" in Meryle Secrest's *Somewhere for Me*, p. 325. Mrs. Rodgers was explaining why she wanted to have a rabbi on hand during her daughter's interfaith marriage.

4. Ewen, *Richard Rodgers*, p. 32.

5. Hyland, *George Gershwin*, p. 213.

6. Ibid., p. 210.

7. Patricia Erens, *The Jew in American Cinema* (Bloomington: Indiana University Press, 1984), and particularly her discussion of the film *Gentleman's Agreement*, p. 178.

8. Herman Wouk wrote the novel *Marjorie Morningstar*, which was published in 1955. The movie came out three years later.

9. See Most, *Making Americans*, for an astute analysis of the "politics of race" in *South Pacific*.

10. Pollack, *George Gershwin*, p. 11.

11. Lahr, "Come Rain or Come Shine," p. 90.

12. Ira Gershwin quoted in Jablonski, *Harold Arlen*, p. 89.

13. As paraphrased by Jeffrey Melnick, *A Right to Sing the Blues: African Americans, Jews, and American Popular Song* (Cambridge, Mass: Harvard University Press, 1999), p. 185.

14. John Leland, *Hip: The History* (New York: Ecco Press, 2004), p. 203.

15. Pollack, *George Gershwin*, pp. 49, 127.

16. Wyatt and Johnson, *George Gershwin Reader*, p. 124.

17. Melnick, *A Right to Sing the Blues*, p. 103.

18. Ibid., pp. 119, 128.

19. Michael Alexander, *Jazz Age Jews* (Princeton, N.J.: Princeton University Press, 2001), p. 170.

20. Irving Howe, *World of Our Fathers* (New York: Simon and Schuster, 1976), p. 563.

21. Kurt List put a lot of these ideas in his article "Jerome Kern and American Operetta," *Commentary* (May 1947), pp. 433–441.

22. Leonard Bernstein, "Why Don't You Run Upstairs and Write a Nice Gershwin Tune?" (1955), in *The George Gershwin Reader*, pp. 298–99.

23. Quoted in Pollack, *George Gershwin*, p. 625.

24. David Remnick, "The Joshua Generation," *The New Yorker*, November 17, 2008, pp. 69–70, 72.

25. Accounts vary. Moshe Reuben Yoelson, father of Al, has been thought to be a rabbi, a cantor, a *shochet* (one who slaughters animals in the prescribed manner), and a *mohel* (one who performs the ritual of circumcision).

26. Tormé, *My Singing Teachers*, p. 118.

27. Gary Giddins, "Changing the Face of America," *New York Sun*, October 23, 2007.

28. Alexander, *Jazz Age Jews.* p, 176.

29. David Schiff, *Gershwin: Rhapsody in Blue* (New York: Cambridge University Press, 1997), p. 98.

30. Robert Gottlieb, ed., *Reading Dance* (New York: Pantheon, 2008), p. 62.

31. As quoted in Wilk, *They're Playing Our Song*, p. 25.

VIII. Some Other Time

1. The Yankees played the Brooklyn Dodgers in 1949, 1952, 1953, 1955, and 1956. They took on the New York Giants in 1951. In 1962 and 1963 the Yankees competed for baseball's top prize with the Giants and Dodgers, respectively, but by then those teams represented San Francisco and Los Angeles. The Yankees also played in the World Series in 1950, 1957, 1958, 1960, 1961, and 1964. The Giants won the Series in 1954, the Dodgers in 1959.

2. Music by Jerome Kern. The line is from a stanza contributed by Oscar Hammerstein. Most of the lyric was written by P. G. Wodehouse for a 1918 show called *Oh, Lady! Lady!* But the song was dropped and went unheard until *Show Boat* hit the stage in 1927.

3. Meryle Secrest, *Leonard Bernstein: A Life* (New York: Vintage, 1995), p. 118.

4. Bernstein, *The Joy of Music*, pp. 61–62.

5. Artur Rodzinski: "When Bernstein was just getting started, Otto Klemperer came by to hear a rehearsal. While the orchestra was playing, Bernstein sat listening and following the score—I was conducting—but even to Klemperer this upstart would not hand over his copy of the score. So Klemperer had to lean over Bernstein's chair to follow the score Bernstein was holding. Even in those days he was a terribly fresh guy. Ever heard the Jewish word 'chutzpah'? It roughly means a fresh and aggressive guy with lots of guts, and it fits Bernstein exactly." Joan Peyser, *Bernstein: A Biography* (New York: Morrow, 1987), p. 114.

6. Ibid., pp. 139, 143.

7. Ibid., p. 23.

8. George Gershwin suggested to Dukelsky that he name himself Vernon Duke. In addition to the popular songs ("I Can't Get Started," "Taking a Chance on Love") that he wrote as Vernon Duke, the Russian-born composer continued to write symphonies, concertos, ballets—as well as poetry—under his birth name.

9. Peyser, *Bernstein*, p. 197.

10. Ibid., p. 437.

ACKNOWLEDGMENTS

Jonathan Rosen is a brilliant editor and I am fortunate to have had his guidance. Hannah Oberman-Breindel went through the manuscript and made many valuable suggestions. Rahel Lerner prepared the chronology. Friends, too many to list without fear of inadvertently omitting a name, have helped me immensely with their thoughts and encouragement. I should single out the contributions of my agent, Glen Hartley, and of Dan Frank of Pantheon. My wife, Stacey, is my first and best reader, and this book is dedicated to her.

The stanzas from May Swenson's poem "An Exuberance, Not a Dump" are reprinted with permission of The Literary Estate of May Swenson. Many thanks to Carole Berglie. The lines from Brad Leithauser's "A Good List" are reprinted with permission of the poet.

ABOUT THE AUTHOR

David Lehman is the author of *Signs of the Times: Deconstruction and the Fall of Paul de Man*, the editor of *The Oxford Book of American Poetry*, and the series editor of *The Best American Poetry*. His books of poetry include *The Daily Mirror*, *When a Woman Loves a Man*, and the forthcoming *Yeshiva Boys*. He has also written *The Last Avant-Garde: The Making of the New York School of Poets* and *The Perfect Murder: A Study in Detection*. He has received fellowships from the Guggenheim Foundation and the National Endowment for the Arts, as well as the Award in Literature from the American Academy of Arts and Letters. He has taught in the graduate writing program of the New School in New York City since the program's inception in 1996. He lives in New York City.